# The Complete Dales Walker

## 2. The Southern Dales

### Colin Speakman

DALESMAN

**Dalesman Publishing Company Limited,**
Stable Courtyard, Broughton Hall,
Skipton, North Yorkshire BD23 3AE


**First Published 1994**


Text © 1994 Colin Speakman
Maps © 1994 David W. Holdsworth

Cover: Appletreewick by Deryck Hallam


Typeset by Lands Services
Printed by Lavenham Press


A British Library Cataloguing in Publication
record is available for this book


**ISBN 1 85568 071 8**

Every effort has been made to ensure that information given on
walks is accurate and up to date. Readers must seek permission
where necessary to use footpaths and refer to the appropriate
up-to-date Ordnance Survey maps for more detailed guidance.
Details of recent footpath diversions can usually be obtained from
National Park and tourist information centres.

# CONTENTS

# INTRODUCTION

THIS book brings together a collection of popular circular walks in the southern part of the Yorkshire Dales which were first published during the 1980s as three separate small Dalesman paperbacks: *Walking in the Three Peaks*, *Walks in Malhamdale* and *Walks in Upper Wharfedale*.

All are circular walks, reflecting the fact that more than 90 per cent of walks in the Yorkshire Dales are undertaken to or from a parked car. However, all are accessible by public transport, either by train or bus, and an indication of appropriate services as well as car parking is given in the text. This is not only designed to help people without access to a car, but to encourage drivers to consider more environmentally friendly ways of travel and, an increasingly important factor in many rural areas, as an alternative to leaving a parked car in a remote rural car park, vulnerable to car crime.

Most are fairly short walks, designed for a half rather than a full day's walk, and are aimed less at the experienced hiker than the casual walker or newcomer to rambling. Whilst some less well-known walks have been included, it was felt important to include some of the more famous and well-known places because a guide-book which didn't include at least some of the highlights is hardly doing its job.

The downside of this is that it includes walks which have, over recent years with the rapid increase in the popularity of walking and a dramatic increase in the number of guidebooks published, become very busy. In a few areas, most notably along parts of the Three Peaks Walk, this has led to problems of footpath erosion.

Where possible such areas have been avoided. In some places expensive remedial work has had to be undertaken by the National Park Authority. Walkers can help by keeping to clear, waymarked paths and following any directional signs to help reduce wear and tear on the countryside. Such problems, serious as they are in a few places, can, however, be exaggerated, and also reflect a welcome increased use and enjoyment of the Yorkshire Dales countryside by many thousands of people. This usage has a direct economic benefit in terms of a flourishing tourism industry in the region – an industry upon which the welfare of many Dales families increasingly depends. Most of the Dales, as users of this book will testify, remain extremely quiet, with certain areas, even in Ribblesdale and Malhamdale, with under-used paths and almost forgotten ways which yet remain to be explored.

## The Yorkshire Dales National Park

All the walks in this book lie within the Yorkshire Dales National Park. This, the third largest of Britain's eleven National Parks, covers 680 square miles of spectacular central Pennine scenery, its peaks rising to over 700 metres – 2,300 feet. It is an area which contains much of the finest limestone scenery in the British Isles, and also vast areas of gritstone and heather moorlands cut through by steep-sided valleys where rivers run through richly fertile pastureland, becks and streams tumbling down in spectacular waterfalls.

Despite its name, the National Park is neither nationally owned nor is it a park; unlike most European and American National Parks this is a lived-in, occupied landscape, a countryside of small farms and villages, as well as some larger estates. Most land is privately owned, and whilst the landscape receives national protection through the work of the National Park Authority, visitors have exactly the same access rights as anywhere else in Britain – that is along the excellent network of public rights of way, footpaths and bridleways, that criss-cross the area. Over certain areas, such as the magnificent Barden Moor and Fell Access Areas in Upper Wharfedale, an Access Agreement allows walkers – without dogs – to enjoy freedom to roam subject to various byelaws and restriction at times of fire risk or on a limited number of shooting days.

Visitors to the Yorkshire Dales National Park are warmly welcome, and throughout this book walkers will see evidence of maintenance work on footpaths and bridleways undertaken by the National Park's Area Management Service – as the warden service is now known – which makes pathfinding so much easier and reduces the risk of accidental trespass. All of the work of the National Park is undertaken in close co-operation with farmers and landowners, planting trees, conserving wildlife habitats, removing eyesores and preventing unsightly development.

It is a landscape rich in natural beauty and in human and historical associations. Bird lovers and botanists will find enormous variety to enjoy, whilst the geology of the Park is nationally famous. But equally fascinating is the human dimension – the living archaeology of the landscape, traces of Bronze Age and Iron Age field systems, patterns of Anglian and Viking settlement, monastic remains and medieval walls. There is also an extraordinary industrial heritage, especially lead mining, which leaves its visible traces on much moorland, and in the stone villages built to serve its industrial communities, paradoxically now among the most picturesque tourist centres.

The more one understands about the Yorkshire Dales the more one enjoys even the shortest walk. National Park Centres at Grassington, Malham, Clapham, Aysgarth, Hawes and Sedbergh offer not only informative displays but a wide range of books and pamphlets which give insight into the local and natural history far beyond the scope of this guide. Some recommended further reading is also included at the end of this section.

Please remember wherever you go in the Yorkshire Dales to

respect the life and work of the countryside. Farmers in heavily visited areas of the Dales suffer nuisance and disturbance from a minority of visitors. Keep to footpaths and bridleways across enclosed land, and if you have a dog, please keep it on a lead, especially during lambing time which can be any time between the end of February and early May. Close gates behind you unless they are clearly meant to be propped open, and keep in single file across meadowland. Take all litter back home with you – remember the American National Park's adage to "take only photographs and leave only footprints".

# Some practical points

This guide is intended to supplement and not to replace the careful use of large-scale maps. No verbal guide can give the kind of exact information a good map supplies. Words help supply some extra information, and will help you select a route, but maps are the essential first step.

Three excellent Ordnance Survey Outdoor Leisure Maps at 1:25,000 scale cover the whole of the Yorkshire Dales and every walk in this book. These are No.10 *Yorkshire Dales Western Area* (Ribblesdale and the Three Peaks), No.10 *Yorkshire Dales Southern Area* (Malhamdale and Central and Upper Wharfedale as far as Kettlewell), and No.30 *Yorkshire Dales Central and Northern Area* (Upper Wharfedale north of Kettlewell and Langstrothdale).

Also useful, and in many ways easier to use, being based on careful survey work by a dedicated walker, are Arthur Gemmell's excellent Stile Maps series, including Bolton Abbey, Grassington, Three Peaks, and Malhamdale. All are on sale in local shops and in National Park Centres.

Do not go out onto the hills without being properly equipped. Some of these walks involve climbing to wild, remote areas, some of them to countryside as wild and bleak as anything in Britain, where weather conditions can, without warning, change to extremes. Always carry waterproofs, warm clothing, emergency food, a compass you can use, and, in the winter months, a torch. Boots are essential for even the shortest of these walks. Paths are often wet and muddy and limestone pavements, crossed on several of these walks, can be slippy even for the well shod. Modern light-weight boots will give comfortable support and are a worthwhile investment.

Any problems on footpaths should be reported, giving exact details of the nature of the obstruction or problems, and if possible a map reference, to the National Park Officer, Yorkshire Dales National Park, Colvend, Grassington, Skipton, North Yorkshire, BD23 5LB.

Public transport information is available from British Rail (enquiries tel. 0532 448133) or the three major bus operators in the area, Keighley and District Travel (0535 603284), Pennine Motors (0756 749215) and Ribble Motor Service (0524 64228). Invaluable for public transport information about the whole of the Dales is Dales Connections, a pocket timetable of all bus and rail services, available from National Parts Centres and Tourist Information Centres in the area or in case of difficulty send 60p in stamps to Elmtree Press, The Elms, Exelby, Bedale, North Yorkshire, DL8 2HD.

Two organisations every reader of this guide should be interested in supporting are the Ramblers' Association and the Yorkshire Dales Society.

The Ramblers' Association, the national body which campaigns for footpaths and for access to the countryside, has an active local branch – the West Riding Area – covering the southern part of the Yorkshire Dales. The association's address is 1/5 Wandsworth Road, London, SW8 2XX.

The Yorkshire Dales Society is a charity concerned to protect the unique landscape and cultural heritage of the Yorkshire Dales, working closely with the Council for National Parks and other organisations at a national and local level, as well as having a quarterly magazine and a programme of Dales-based events exploring many different aspects of the Dales heritage. The society's address is The Civic Centre, Cross Green, Otley, West Yorkshire, LS21 1HD.

# Further reading

Norman Duerden: *Portrait of the Dales* (Hale, 1978).
Peter Gunn: *The Yorkshire Dales: A Landscape with Figures* (Century, 1984).
Marie Hartley and Joan Ingilby: *The Yorkshire Dales* (Dent, 1964).
F.W. Houghton: *Upper Wharfedale* (Dalesman, 1980).
W.R. Mitchell: *The Changing Dales* (Dalesman, 1988).
Richard Muir: *The Dales of Yorkshire: A Portrait* (Macmillan, 1991).
Arthur Raistrick: *Old Yorkshire Dales* (David & Charles, 1967).
Arthur Raistrick: *The Pennine Dales* (Eyre Methuen, 1968).
Arthur Raistrick: *Malham and Malham Moor* (Dalesman, 1965).
Arthur Raistrick: *Mines and Miners on Malham Moor* (Yorkshire Dales National Park, 1977).
Harry Rée and Caroline Forbes: *The Three Peaks of Yorkshire* (Wildwood, 1983).
Colin Speakman: *Walking in the Yorkshire Dales* (Hale, 1983).
Colin Speakman: *A Portrait of North Yorkshire* (Hale, 1986).
Tony Waltham: *Yorkshire Dales National Park* (Webb & Bower, 1987).

# Central and Upper Wharfedale

WHARFEDALE is undoubtedly the most heavily visited of the major Yorkshire Dales. This is no doubt in part owing to its close proximity to the big West Yrokshire conurbations of Leeds and Bradford, but also because it is so astonishingly beautiful, a landscape of grandeur dominated by high fell country and yet having extraordinary intimacy within the enclosed valley itself.

The River Wharfe is arguably one of the loveliest of all English rivers, squeezing its way in central Wharfedale between two massive areas of gritstone moorland – Barden Moor and Barden Fell. This entire area forms part of the great Bolton Abbey Estate. Bolton Priory itself, and its riverside and surrounding woodlands and magnificent heather moorlands, have for many years been open to the public, the moorlands through the mechanism of an access agreement between the estate and the Yorkshire Dales National Park.

Recreation and conservation have dominated this area since medieval times. It was a great hunting estate in the days of the Lord Cliffords and the Earls of Cumberland; in the 18th and 19th centuries ornamental woodlands and parkland were laid out, walks through the woods created and heather moorland burned and managed. Visitors have long been welcome to share a landscape which has delighted poet and painter, sportsman and aesthete, for generations.

Beyond Burnsall the limestone country begins – a more open landscape with scattered villages, ancient limestone pastures whose Anglian terraces patterns are still discernible, as well as industry in the form of the remains of moorland lead mining and modern limestone quarries.

In Upper Wharfedale, beyond Grassington, a different kind of landscape begins to emerge, bleaker and wilder, where the valley narrows above the great crag at Kilnsey. The river valley twists its way between high, bleak fells, past the confluence with the Skirfare which threads down Littondale, past the old mining settlement of Kettlewell, to Buckden, once a small forest community in the medieval hunting forest of Langstrothdale. Much of this area forms part of a magnificent estate, thanks to a generous gift by Mr Graham Watson, which is now largely owned and managed by the National Trust as a specially protected part of the heartland of the Yorkshire Dales National Park.

# Haw Pike

*This walk on the edge of the National Park to a less well known summit offers exceptionally fine panoramic views of central Wharfedale, without having to climb great heights. Time required: 2-2½ hours.*

*Parking: Because Addingham has no official public car park, park in Bark Lane on the Bolton Abbey road from Ilkley just beyond Addingham Church where there is a wide tarmac verge and safe parking on the roadside near to Addingham suspension bridge – the end of the walk.*

*Public Transport: Hourly buses from Leeds, Skipton (service 783, 784), Ilkley (Services 784, 765) and from Keighley (765, 762). Alight at The Fleece and walk towards Skipton before turning right up Sugar Hill (lane by public conveniences) to join the walk by the old railway line.*

*Refreshment: A choice of pubs and cafes in the village.*

*Map: OS Pathfinder SE05/15 Bolton Abbey and Blubberhouses; OS Outdoor Leisure Sheet 10 (Yorkshire Dales Southern Area) (part only)*

WALK along Bark Lane in the Bolton Abbey direction to the junction with the B6160 from Addingham village centre. Cross and turn left and almost immediately turn right into Springfield Road, a narrow lane by the backs of houses and gardens. At the end keep straight ahead by more gardens to continue down an alleyway leading to a stile and tiny pedestrian gate. Cross here into a field, but bear left across a farm track to a tall wooden gap stile in the fence on the left. This gives access to a narrow stony path which crosses to the old Ilkley-Bolton-Abbey railway line – an early and much lamented victim of the Beeching axe in 1965. Turn left alongside what remains of the old railway embankment to emerge by an old railway bridge where Sugar Hill, the lane from the centre of Addingham to be used for anyone coming by bus, joins the route.

Turn right here but take the first track again to the right, signposted by a cottage which soon passes a school. Just past a ruined barn a kissing gate, left, signed, indicates the line of the path which follows the edge of the fields alongside the farm track.

This is a steady, but easy, climb rewarded by magnificent views of Beamsley Beacon to your right, the conical summit which in Tudor times was one of the great chain of beacons used to alert

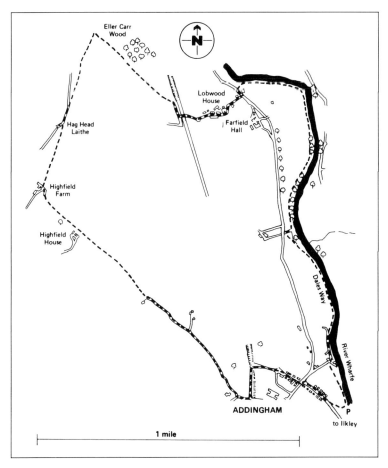

communities to major events or warn them of threats such as the Spanish Armada of 1588.

The path continues alongside the farmtrack which soon becomes an overgrown way. Eventually you are in a narrow field. Keep ahead, over two more stiles heading towards a fine Georgian farm, Highfield House, ahead. The next stile is over the fence ahead, immediately to the right and behind the farm. Keep ahead with a wire fence to your right to the next stile in the stone wall ahead, by the gate. The path now heads towards Highfield Farm, but before the farm bear right to a stile marked with white paint in the wall by the wall corner.

Your way is now in the same direction across a shallow dip in the pasture ahead to a steep step stile you will see in the wall directly ahead. The next stile, by a ruined barn, is murderously steep and should be only tackled by the most agile, the better part of valour being to bear left around the edge of the wall by the ruin. This low hill is Haw Pike, though the actual summit trig point is some distance to the left.

The way is now to the right along a green track through a gate, but in the next field bear right away from the track to the wall corner where there is another stone step stile – this time with a magnificent view of the dale, with Simons Seat, Bolton Bridge and Bolton Abbey itself as well as the whole sweep of the River Wharfe in a matchless setting spread out before you.

The path now descends to open pasture in the same direction towards a wood in the dip of the hill – Lob Wood – but after about 200 metres where the path is intersected by a path from the right (not visible on the ground), veer sharp right towards the wall corner. This emerges immediately above another little wood – Eller Carr Wood – below, where you'll see a steepish step stile just above the wall corner (which can be avoided by going to the field gate to the right).

Cross now to the bottom corner of the next field. Here the path goes through a gate and close to the old railway line once again to a second gate and a track, left, under the buttresses of an old railway bridge. This leads to Lobwood House Farm. Keep to the right of the large new cow house and along the farm drive to the main B6160 road.

Cross extremely carefully (there is no pavement and traffic travels fast) to turn left and face the oncoming traffic for a few metres to a stile immediately to the left of a house leading into woodland by the riverside. This soon crosses two stiles and follows pasture along the River Wharfe through Low Park – part of the Dales Way, the popular 81-mile route that links the Yorkshire Dales and the Lake District from Ilkley to Windermere. There are fine views both across the riverside and back to Ilkley Moor, with its twin summit wireless masts a notable landmark ahead.

The path crosses two more stiles before climbing wooden steps and emerging on the road by Fairfield House where the next section of route immediately starts, again going along the riverside. At High Mill continue past the caravan site and the old textile mill itself, now converted into riverside homes. The path climbs to the suspension bridge and Bark Lane. Anyone heading for the centre of Addingham for refreshment, toilets and public transport should turn left; but then go first right along Church Lane to Main Street and the village centre.

# Bolton Priory

*A famous walk by one of England's most beautiful ecclesiastical ruins, too fine to omit from any book of walks in Upper Wharfedale, particularly recommended in the winter months when the return riverside walk is less likely to be shared with lines of parked cars. Time required: 1½-2 hours.*

*Terrain: Easy woodland and riverside paths.*

*Parking: Large public car park at Bolton Abbey on the B6160 road from Ilkley and Addingham.*

*Public Transport: Weekday services from Skipton and Grassington Bus Stations (Keighley & District service 76); summer weekend Dalesbus services from Leeds and Ilkley (Dalesbus 800), plus limited Sunday services from certain Lancashire towns – Leisurelink.*

*Refreshment: Bolton Abbey – cafe at post office; cafeteria with choice of meals and snacks at Cavendish Pavilion – half way point.*

*Map: OS Outdoor Leisure Sheet 10 (Yorkshire Dales Southern Area); OS Pathfinder SE05/15 Bolton Abbey and Blubberhouses. Stile Maps: Bolton Abbey Footpath Map.*

FROM the Bolton Abbey car park make your way to the top and out by the information board kiosk (toilets nearby). Bear right along the lane to the main road where, opposite the junction, the "hole in the wall" gateway leads to that first magnificent view of Bolton Priory in its setting on a buff of land within a great arc of the river.

Go down the steps and along the path – but if you choose to visit the priory before the walk (you pass it again on the return journey) branch left to the stile in the fence which runs alongside the main drive down to the priory church.

Though the village is known as Bolton Abbey, the famous ruins set in such immaculate parkland are actually the surviving portions of an Augustinian priory, dating from the 12th century. They contain work right up to the 16th century when Prior Richard Moone was forced to surrender his community to Thomas Cromwell on 29th January 1539, leaving his great west tower, which forms the entrance to the church, unfinished.

Fortunately, the beautiful priory church survives and continues, as it has for many centuries, as the parish church for the village community of Bolton Abbey. It welcomes thousands of visitors each year – local guides are on duty at busy times and will explain architectural and other details.

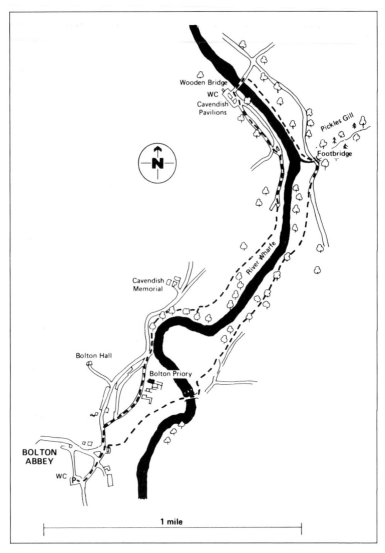

The splendours of the ancient church and its associated ruins have attracted enthusiasts of the picturesque for over two hundred years, among them such giants of the English Romantic movement as the poet Wordsworth, the painters Girtin, Cox, Turner and Landseer and the Victorian art critic and moralist John Ruskin.

Bolton Abbey has also, for successive generations, been the focal point of the Yorkshire estates of the Dukes of Devonshire, and the great and famous, including prime ministers and monarchs (King George V was a frequent guest) have stayed in the handsome Gothic shooting lodge converted from the gatehouse, opposite the priory.

When you have had time thoroughly to explore the priory church and ruins, make your way through the little gate to the far side of the graveyard and walk down to cross the footbridge (or parallel stepping stones) across the River Wharfe. At the other side, take the path which nears slightly to the right, up steps.

Keep on the main path which follows the hillside into the Priory Woods – ignoring the path, signed to Storiths, which zigzags to the right.

There are magnificent views back to the priory ruins from here with, if the river runs calmly, fine reflections in the water. The paths through the woods have recently been restored. They were originally laid out as ornamental walks for visitors around 150 years ago by a remarkable vicar of Bolton Abbey – the Reverend William Carr, a noted scholar whose claims to fame included the first ever Yorkshire dialect dictionary and the breeding of the oversized "Craven Heifer", which is still to be seen in local inn signs.

Keep on along the main path which follows a man-made shelf through the woods before emerging at the lane above Pickles Gill – a footbridge across the beck here will save you getting wet feet in the ford. Turn left and follow the beck back to the riverside.

A stile in the wall corner on the right gives access to the riverside path leading to the recently restored wooden bridge at Cavendish Pavilion – a welcoming cafeteria which is open for most of the year including winter weekends. There are toilets nearby.

You can, if you've time and energy, more than double the length of this walk by following one of a choice of waymarked trails through Strid Woods (entrance by the pavilion), continuing as far as Barden Tower. A map of the trails can be obtained at the pavilion.

The route back is along the drive up from the Cavendish Pavilion but almost immediately bear left to the riverside. Keep along by the river for about half a mile, past the end of the car park, before bearing right to where a steep path, with steps, leads out of the field corner and to the entrance of the pavilion drive on the B6160, next to the Gothic fountain. This was built as a memorial to Lord Frederick Cavendish, heir to the Devonshire estates, who was murdered by Irish nationalists in Phoenix Park, Dublin, in 1882.

Continue ahead to where the path, parallel to the road, crosses a wooden footbridge over a ravine, and leads to the gate and entrance to Bolton Priory from the opposite side. Continue past the Priory and along the drive, taking the stile in the fence, left, which leads back up to the "hole in the wall" and the car park.

# Halton Heights

*A walk on the edge of Barden Moor offering some magnificent high-level views of the dale, returning by field path, specially recommended in late summer when the heather on the moors is a rich shade of purple. Time required: 3 hours.*

*Terrain: Rough moorland tracks and field paths and a steady uphill climb of half a mile at the end of the walk. Boots advised. Because of the nature of the start of the walk across open country, it is not recommended in times of poor visibility such as mist or low cloud.*

*Parking: Free informal parking places at Halton Heights just past the cattle grid on the Skipton-Embsay-Barden road. From Skipton follow Embsay signs and continue beyond Eastby to Halton Heights. From the B6160 Addingham-Burnsall road turn left just before Barden Tower to reach the car part on the summit of the hill.*

*Public Transport: Keighley & District service 76 from Skipton bus station to Eastby – start the walk at Eastby. (More frequent service to and from Embsay, one mile from Eastby, by Keighley & District service 75).*

*Refreshment: Eastby (Inn).*

*Map: OS Outdoor Leisure Sheet 10 (Yorkshire Dales Southern Area); OS Pathfinder SE05/15 Bolton Abbey and Blubberhouses.*

BARDEN Moor and Fell constitute one of the finest areas of unspoiled heather moorland in the North of England to which there is legal public access. However the moor is closed on certain days of the year for shooting between August and December – never on Sundays – and at times of high fire risk. Though this walk largely uses public rights of way on the moor, it is not advisable to do this walk at such times – notices are posted on the moor to warn walkers. Dogs are not permitted on the moor, but if dog owners take care to keep strictly to the rights of way as shown on the Outdoor Leisure or Pathfinder Map and keep their dogs under control, they are perfectly within their rights on the public path.

From the car park, head along the obvious stony track which starts just west of the cattle grid (the right of way begins another 100 metres to the south) and bear westwards over the moor. This is a fairly level way soon giving quite splendid views across Lower Barden Reservoir and an area of desolately beautiful heather land-scape, stretching away across a great, empty bowl to the summit of the moor. You'll hear the angry chatter of grouse swooping

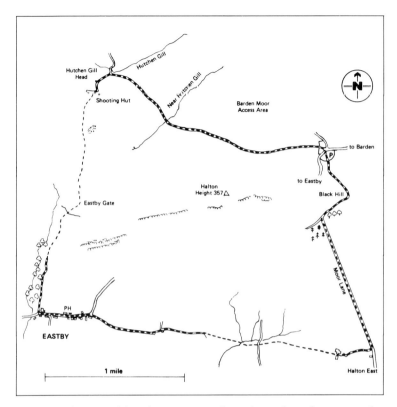

up from clumps of heather at most times hovering above a rocky outcrop looking for lizards or voles.

The track, which is joined by the right-of-way, soon swings round along the contour – avoid a fainter track forking off left but keep on the main way which crosses a stream, near Hutchen Gill, then curves round to a deeper little ravine, Hutchen Gill itself. Just before the gill, a track bears left towards a shooting hut. This is not the public path which only branches off a faint and narrow way some 200 metres to the north. But unless you've a dog with you, most people will prefer the obvious short cut to the shooting hut (strictly private) at Hutchen Gill Head.

Turn left at the hut to locate a narrow path which follows the top of a narrow dyke, east of the shooting butts, heading due south across the moorland. Again this more obvious and better used route diverts slightly from the right of way. Head just to the right of the line of crags – Eastby Crag – you will see ahead. A large plantation forms a further landmark to the left, with the more spectacular conical summit of Embsay Crag further to the right.

The path peters out in moorland grass, but you should be able to see a gate and ladder stile ahead – Eastby Gate – which leads off the moor.

Cross the stile and you enter an enclosed green lane with further stiles ahead, bearing slightly right. There are fine views from here across the narrow shoulder of land which separates Wharfedale and Airedale, crossed by the main A59 and A65 roads by Draughton. Haw Pikes quarries are to the left and, if it happens to be a Sunday, Embsay Steam Railway's little steam locomotive with its trailing coaches is clearly in view as it puffs along to Holywell Halt. Keep ahead, your way marked by stiles, down a little ravine, Heigh Gill. The path soon crosses a stile to enter a wood, extremely picturesque if somewhat muddy, with a little waterfall to your right.

You emerge by cottages into the lane at Eastby – turn left along the main street, past the village pub, but where the road swings left towards Barden, keep directly ahead along Bark Lane, an unmetalled track. Continue, through gates, as the way becomes a pleasant field path beyond the evocatively named barn, Angrymire Laithe. Keep in the same direction, the path going along the edge of fields, the way now marked by stiles, soon crossing Berry Ground Beck at a little footbridge and following the far side of the stream over more stiles.

You soon find yourself in a large open field – head towards a stile slightly to the right and towards the farm ahead. Go through a gate at the farm, turning right through and between farm buildings then left on to the main farm drive – closing gates behind you. The farm drive brings you to a cross roads. Turn left here, into Moor Lane, a broad green way which as its name implies is an ancient access way to the moor.

You have a steady uphill climb now, but take time to pause and catch your breath and turn back to enjoy impressive views across Draughton and Skipton Moor. At the top gate follow the track to the right, round the edge of Black Hill, to car parks below Halton Height.

# Thorpe in the Hollow

*This is a favourite walk between two of the most perfectly situated villages in Upper Wharfedale, along paths that offer exceptionally fine views. Time required: 2 hours.*

*Terrain: Field paths and a section of riverside. Quite a number of stiles to negotiate – not a walk to be hurried.*

*Parking: In the public car park by the riverside at Burnsall.*

*Public Transport: Keighley & District service 76 from Skipton or from Grassington bus station to Burnsall (weekdays only). Service 800 (Dalesbus) at weekends April-October, direct from Ilkley, Bradford and Leeds.*

*Refreshment: Burnsall – choice of cafes and two inns. Toilets by the car park.*

*Map: OS Outdoor Leisure Sheet 10 (Yorkshire Dales Southern Area); OS Pathfinder SE06/16 Grassington and Pateley Bridge. Stile Maps: Grassington Footpath Map.*

IT IS difficult to imagine a better setting for a village than Burnsall enjoys – where the River Wharfe, having been forced into a deep limestone ravine, opens out into a green and sheltered south-facing valley, protected on all sides by 1,500 feet high fells. The village has a medieval church with two Anglo-Viking "hog-back" grave-stones, a 17th century grammar school now used as the local primary school, a riverside village green complete with maypole, and a scatter of cottages and small houses which create a perfect harmony with the wild fell country all around. The handsome bridge was last rebuilt in the 19th century, after being destroyed by floods. Following a similar occurrence in the 17th century the bill was paid by Sir William Craven, the "Dick Whittington of the Dales" who left his native Appletreewick eventually to become Lord Mayor of London. As well as restoring the bridge, be rebuilt the church and built and endowed the grammar school.

From Burnsall car park walk to the crossroads by the Red Lion, keeping left along the Grassington road, following the road as it bears sharp right. Just past the corner, by a stone horse trough, a gate by a wooden footpath sign leads across a small stone flagged yard to another gate. Go through both by the edge of a garden to a stile leading into a field.

The path is now marked by a series of low step stiles across the fields, some with little lambing gates above them. Notice how the

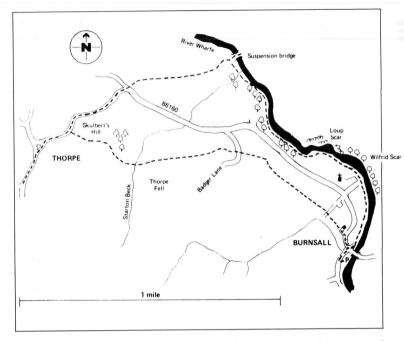

stiles are of a darker sandstone contrasting to the pale limestone of the rest of the walls. This is because the path lies close to the major fault lines where the newer darker sandstones yield to the paler Great Scar limestones giving a pepper-and-salt effect to the walls.

Keep ahead through stiles across a farmtrack and over more stiles through small fields. To your left rises the massive bulk of Thorpe Fell – part of the Barden Moor Access Area – forming an impressive skyline.

Soon after the path crosses another farmtrack you find yourself in a broader field, close to a line of wooden pylons, with a triangular section of drystone wall ahead of you. Keep to the right of the apex of this triangle to locate a stile a few yards to the right. The way now crosses another farmtrack, Badger Lane, and along a wall – fine views to the right across the valley to the village of Hebden with its church. As the path dips, look for a signpost near the wall indicating the way which now bears left up the pasture, close to two ash trees, dipping down again to a ladder stile. Cross to the next stile, the way now descending to a little plank bridge over a stream, Starton Beck. Follow the way up by the wall which encloses a small wood, going through a gate and bearing slightly left to a ladder stile. This enters a green lane.

Follow this to the junction with the metalled lane into Thorpe.

Thorpe in the Hollow, or Thorpe-sub-montem to give it its latinate name, was known as the hidden village because according to legend it escaped the depredations of 14th century Scottish raiders. They reputedly passed down the dale not knowing of the village's existence, situated as it is in a tight hollow of the hills. In medieval times it was reputed to be a centre of shoemakers – a cobbler was at work here up until about a century ago.

Little else has changed here since last century, and as you arrive in the village there's a magnificent 18th century farmhouse on your right and two handsome barns, with neo-classical features, on the left. The road through the village becomes a track and then a moorland path over the shoulder of Elbolton Hill with its caves where a number of important archaeological finds were made in the last century.

To return to Burnsall, retrace your steps along the lane out of Thorpe, but keep ahead over the brow of the hill past the point where the green lane branches off, soon dropping down into the main valley towards the main road. The views are extensive – to the right you'll see Grass Wood and beyond Old Cote Moor, Buckden Pike and Great Whernside, Grassington Moor and, just discernible above Hebden Gill, Grassington Moor Lead Mines' Chimney. The crag above the felltop to the south west is Simons Seat.

At the main road cross immediately to a ladder stile and a bridle-way signed to Hebden. Follow the wall to another stile, descending now to a gateway marked with blue bridgeway waymarks, and follow a line of posts taking you down to the little suspension bridge over the Wharfe, leading to Hebden below. This bridge was originally made just over 100 years ago by the local blacksmith who constructed the bridge in pieces for it to be erected on site and tensioned by wires – a quite remarkable achievement. It was recently rebuilt by the National Park.

Do not cross but turn left along a quite superb stretch of sheltered path by the river Wharfe – part of the Dales Way. Soon across a stile and a little footbridge the Way follows the river past Loup Scar, a high crag of exposed limestone, climbing a little grassy knoll before returning to the riverside where mallards and the occasional swan are to be seen. Another fine limestone escarpment is passed before coming into the village behind the Red Lion inn car park. You can return to the car park by going down steps at and under the bridge, crossing riverside cobbles to make your way back up the little embankment and on to the village green. There are few nicer ways to end a walk.

# Linton and Threshfield

*A walk from Grassington to take in two attractive neighbouring villages – Threshfield and Linton – with opportunity to enjoy some unusually fine views of this historic landscape. Time required: 2-2½ hours.*

*Terrain: Field paths and tracks. Two short uphill sections. Boots advised – some places can be muddy after rain.*

*Parking: In the National Park car park on Hebden Road (Pateley Bridge road) out of Grassington. Alternative car park available on the road to Linton Church – this shortens the walk by half a mile.*

*Public Transport: Keighley & District service 71 or 72 from Skipton bus station to Grassington; Service 800 (Dalesbus) at weekends April-October from Ilkley, Bradford and Leeds.*

*Refreshment: Grassington – choice of cafes and inns. Toilets by National Park centre. Public houses in both Threshfield and Linton.*

*Map: OS Outdoor Leisure Sheet 10 (Yorkshire Dales Southern Area); OS Pathfinder SE06/16 Grassington and Pateley Bridge. Stile Maps: Grassington Footpath Map.*

FROM the National Park car park and visitor centre, walk across to the far south corner where a wooden kissing gate leads to an enclosed and paved footpath. This is locally known for self-evident reasons as the "Snake Walk" which winds down, through another pedestrian gate, to Linton Falls.

These spectacular falls across the Great Scar limestone mark the point where one of the branches of the Craven Fault – an area of geological fracture – crosses the Wharfe valley. One feature of this walk is the contrast between the paler limestone rocks in the riverside area and the dark, brooding gritstone crags of the high moorland.

For many centuries a watermill existed on this spot, and a former textile mill – Linton Mill – was recently demolished to make way for the new housing development across the river.

Cross the narrow footbridge known as the "Tin Bridge" after an earlier, metal plated structure – the present bridge was recently replaced by the National Park Authority after the previous iron lattice bridge became dangerous. Turn right across the bridge by the houses to the tiny hump-back bridge over Captain Beck – another important former mill stream – to follow the path upstream across the field which soon goes to a short section of wooded riverside.

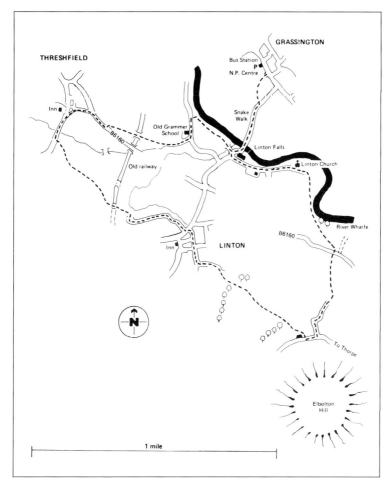

The old brick building on the right by the riverside was, until the 1950s, a hydro-electric station which supplied Grassington with electric power.

The path skirts woodland and emerges into the lane from Linton Church. Turn left here, soon passing the little 17th century Threshfield Grammar School, still in use as the local primary school. Immediately past the school is a field gate on the right. This leads to a footpath along a grassy track which climbs uphill by the wall, soon bearing right to another gate and over the railway bridge which crosses the trackbed of the Yorkshire Dales Railway. Though it closed in 1931 to passenger traffic, the line remained in use until the late 1960s for freight and excursion trains. It still exists as far as the Tilcon Quarry at Swinden with daily trains to steel and cement works.

Continue along the grassy track to the main road at a field gate, turn right to the crossroads and then left along the line into the centre of Threshfield.

Set back behind a busy crossroads, Threshfield is a village which most people go through without stopping or confuse with the spread of suburbia along the main Grassington road. It does have an old centre and little village green surrounded by old cottages and a Manor House which dates from the 17th century, as well as a village inn, The Old Hall.

Unless you are visiting the inn, turn left before the green and walk down to the main road, past the manor house and a barn with its door displaying a rich variety of local horseshoes, to the bridge over the stream. Some 50 metres uphill on the left is a stile. Go through and climb the field to the wall corner where another path is joined by the wallside. Keep left to the next stile, then over the old footbridge over the non-existent railway, before joining a narrow track to Linton. The handsome house on the left linked by stepping stones on the far side of Captain Beck is White Abbey, the former home of the celebrated Dales novelist and topographer Halliwell Sutcliffe.

Linton is one of the most beautiful of all Dales villages. It has a large village green around which the village it situated, crossed by a stream, road, ford and footbridges. The handsome neo-classical building at the far end of the green, reputedly built to the design of the great Sir John Vanbrugh, is Fountains Hospital, an almshouse for local pensioners which is still maintained by the endowment of Richard Fountain, who was born in Linton and became a wealthy Alderman of London where he died in 1725.

Also overlooking the green is the white-walled Fountains Inn, whilst a number of houses and cottages by the green, in quiet side roads and along the main road, all date from the 17th and 18th centuries. Many have the charactertistic mullioned windows and dripstones that were used in the conservative-minded Yorkshire Dales well into the 18th century. Not surprisingly the village is a Conservation Area.

The way continues by crossing the footbridge to the far side of the steam and along to the far end of the village where a farmtrack, left, goes between buildings. The path follows the wall uphill – ignore a ladder stile on the left, but make for the stile ahead. Continue uphill past a narrow section of woodland to the next stile. Then go across a field to a stile immediately to the left of a barn which leads into a narrow lane.

You are now on the side of Elbolton Hill, one of the seven hills of Linton – all of them reef knolls, a rare geological phenomenon consisting of pure deposited limestone, so pure that one of them across the valley, Swinden, has now been totally quarried away for limestone extraction. The views across the valley towards Grassington, Hebden and Grassington Moor are particularly fine. The shallow green terraces visible on the hillside around you and as you begin to descend are raines or lynchets; ancient cultivation terraces which date from Anglican times and mark where arable crops – mainly oats – were grown in terraced fields like modern vineyards.

Turn left in the lane but after about 60 metres a small bridle gate on the left gives access to a beautiful little enclosed bridleway leading down the hillside – this can be overgrown – between walls. Where it ends at a gate, keep slightly left down across the pasture to a gate ahead. A second gate ahead leads to the main road.

Cross with care. Almost immediately to the right is a stile and a further path which bears left through a series of three narrow stiles before entering a large open field, a grassy terrace above the river Wharfe. You see Linton Church below. A ladder stile over the wall below and to the right crosses to a path leading directly to Linton Chutch, joining a path to a stile and a way through the churchyard.

Linton Church, with its little bell tower, dates from the 11th century and is exceptionally interesting in terms of its many Norman and 14th century features. As the ancient parish church of the whole of this part of the dale, it probably occupies a prehistoric site. It has played a major role in the life of the dale over the best part of the last millenium and has many features of exceptional interest. If you visit the church (make sure your boots are clean) you will find a guide on sale.

The road from the church passes the alternative car park and a row of former mill cottages known for reasons which are not entirely certain as "Botany" – probably a link with "Botany Bay" where people were once banished, an ironic reference to the distance people had to walk from Grassington or Linton.

Immediately past the new houses, a passageway leads to the "Tin Bridge" and the "Snake Walk" back to Grassington.

# Grassington and Hebden

*A walk between two popular Dales villages taking advantage of less well-known footpaths that offer some unexpected and interesting views of the upper dale. Time required: 2-2½ hours.*

*Terrain: Pasture and small enclosures with numerous stiles. One uphill section. Boots advised – some places can be muddy after rain.*

*Parking: In the National Park car park on Hebden Road (Pateley Bridge road) out of Grassington.*

*Public Transport: Keighley & District service 71 or 72 from Skipton bus station to Grassington; Service 800 (Dalesbus) at weekends April-October from Ilkley, Bradford and Leeds.*

*Refreshment: Grassington – choice of cafes and inns. Toilets at National Park centre. Hebden – The Clarendon Inn. Toilets at far end of village.*

*Map: OS Outdoor Leisure Sheet 10 (Yorkshire Dales Southern Area); OS Pathfinder SE06/16 Grassington and Pateley Bridge. Stile Maps: Grassington Footpath Map.*

GRASSINGTON, the unofficial capital of Upper Wharfedale, is an excellent starting point for a walk and has a great deal to explore in its own right. You might start your walk by picking up a copy of the Grassington Village Trail from the National Park Centre or local shops; it explains much of the fascinating history of this former lead-mining community.

To begin the main walk, from the National Park Centre go along Hebden Road towards the village centre, turning right into the Square and continuing up Main Street past shops and cafes to the top Square by the Town Hall – the former Mechanics' Institute and still a focal point of the life of the village.

Go right in front of the Town Hall along Low Lane, soon branching left at Garrs End into High Lane – signposted for Hebden. This ancient, sunken track was once an important route to Hebden used by packhorse traffic as its old name "Horse Gap Yett" still indicates. It climbs up and bears right, behind the village, and you are soon looking across rooftops into the valley beyond. After about 200 metres from the junction a metal field gate, about 10 metres before a thorn tree on the left, gives access to a field path not visible on the ground. This crosses to a step stile in the wall on the right, some 30 metres from the wall corner.

Your way is now diagonally across a number of fields, climbing

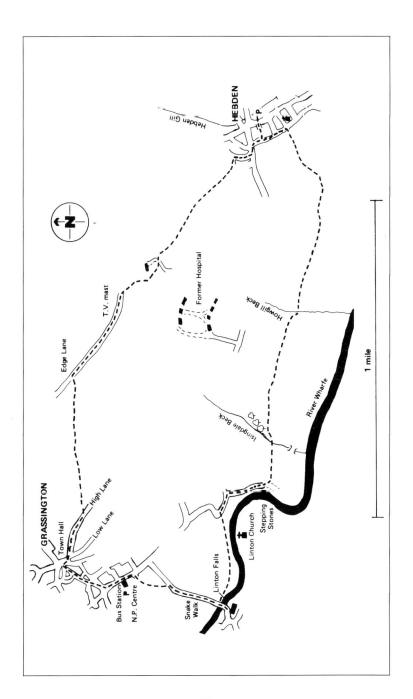

in the direction of the television booster mast you will see ahead, and the one after is in the top right hand corner of the field, with the next immediately behind it. Two more stiles follow, relatively easy to find, before you join a high level enclosed track – Edge Lane – at a gate.

Turn right here, continuing to climb gently uphill towards the television mast. The views are magnificent in every direction – to the north-west, behind you, you'll see Old Cote Moor and Littondale; to the south-west the quarries and the great reef knolls towards Cracoe, then the great expanse of Thorpe Fell and Burnsall Moor (forming part of the Barden Moor Access Area). Ahead of you, as you complete the ascent, is Barden Fell and Simons Seat with the village of Hebden coming into view as you come over the brow of the hill.

Soon past the television mast is a gate and a ladder stile on the right. Cross, descending the pasture above the former Grassington Isolation Hospital, over a little stile ahead and towards a pine wood. The path goes through the edge of the wood to a stile and crossing of paths. Bear left, signed to Hebden, over the stile, going in front of Garnshaw House farm to the stile in the next wall ahead. Again a crossing path, and again you make for Hebden, this time descending through the middle of a broad pasture towards a gap ahead leading to a path which descends by a wall to another stile. The path now bears right across the centre of a long field; make directly for the farm and village ahead. At the bottom of the field a gate leads into a track to a lane. Turn right to reach the main Grassington road by Hargreaves bus garage. The Clarendon Hotel is immediately to your left, as is the village centre around its attractive gill.

Otherwise cross and almost immediately opposite is Brayshaw Lane which leads round the back of this former mining village. Continue to Hebden's little Victorian parish church.

The path back to Grassington begins at the field gate opposite the church and is a historic route – being the ancient parishioners' way from the village to Linton Church used by the people of Hebden before their own church was built in the last century. It is also an exceptionally pretty route with grand views not only of Thorpe Fell and Barden Moor, now seen so clearly in profile, but down into the deep river gorge of the River Wharfe carved out by its ancient glacier.

Your path is in the far right-hand corner of the field, through the farthest of the two gates by a solitary tree. Go along the wall to a steep step stile in the wall corner ahead, then along the wall over another stile as you climb uphill, crossing a narrow pasture to a gap stile. Go right here alongside a ruined wall along another narrow field. Continue alongside the next section of ruined wall ahead to a narrow stile.

Now follow a series of stiles of almost every conceivable type – gap or "squeezer" stiles, step stiles, ladder stiles, little gates – as the path, older than the fields it crosses, follows a high terrace above the river. Just about opposite the end of the former hospital the path, well signed, dog-legs right and then left before following a fence to cross a stream, Howgill Beck, by a welcome National Park boardwalk and footbridge. As you enter open pasture, head for the yellow marker post and the little barn, Ray Laithe, ahead, dropping to another stile through the wall concealed in the hollow. Head to the left of the barn, about 10 metres below which a stile leads to a path which swings left above the wooded Isingdale Beck to another stile.

Cross, bearing right over a little footbridge, and follow the wall, heading towards the riverside. The ancient parishioners' way actually crossed the stepping stones to the 12th century Linton Church, but you'll probably prefer to keep dry feet and go over the stile on the right and along Mill Lane, past Grassington's medieval corn mill (now converted for residential use) and the trout farm. Look at the powerful underground spring at the far side of the farm which drains from Grassington Moor and once powered the furnace bellows of an 18th century lead smeltmill situated at this point.

The path back to Grassington starts from the stile on the left some 50 metres above the trout farm, and again follows a low terrace above the river. Keep ahead at the next stile to the stile by the "Tin Bridge" at Linton Falls – an attractive natural gorge where the Wharfe crosses the limestone outcrops of the Craven Fault. Turn right into the narrow enclosed path known as the "Snake Walk" to the car park and Grassington village.

# Grass Wood

*Grass Wood is that rare jewel – a semi-natural wood on limestone, one of the most beautiful small woods of its kind in the North of England and a nature reserve of national importance. Time required: 2-2½ hours.*

*Terrain: Woodland and riverside paths and tracks. One short uphill section. Boots advised – some places can be muddy after rain.*

*Parking: In the National Park car park on Hebden Road (Pateley Bridge road) out of Grassington.*

*Public Transport: Keighley & District service 71 or 72 from Skipton bus station to Grassington; Service 800 (Dalesbus) at weekends April-October from Ilkley, Bradford and Leeds.*

*Refreshment: Grassington – choice of cafes and inns. Toilets by National Park centre.*

*Map: OS Outdoor Leisure Sheet 10 (Yorkshire Dales Southern Area); OS Pathfinder SE06/16 Grassington and Pateley Bridge. Stile Maps: Grassington Footpath Map.*

FROM the National Park Centre (opposite the bus station) turn left in Hebden Road towards Grassington village but at the cross-roads keep ahead along Wood Lane, passing Grassington Old Hall on your right – a private house but the oldest inhabited building in Wharfedale, dating back to the 18th century.

Continue along Wood Lane. After about 80 metres, turn left into the road known as Raines Meadow, along a road by a new housing estate. As the road bends sharply left, look for steps straight ahead descending to Raines Lane below. Cross and keep ahead to a narrow way by gardens through a kissing gate, crossing a small field to a stile in the wall corner by the end of Grassington Bridge – a low grassy area with a bench, known locally as Donkey Hill.

Don't go up to the road but turn immediately right along the farm track to a kissing gate. This leads to a path that crosses the meadowland to the riverside. Follow the river upstream, soon crossing a stile in the wall and then a little footbridge over a stream. This is a particularly lovely stretch of riverside with the white waters of the Wharfe making a vividly beautiful series of shallow falls set against a backcloth of pale limestone crags and thin woodland.

Follow the path slightly to the right over two step stiles, moving slightly away from the riverside as the path goes along the top of a shallow cliff, with the river in an area of rapids below.

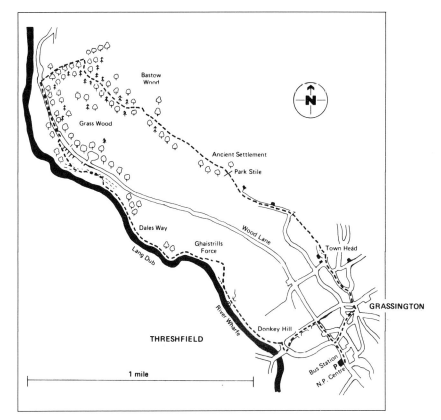

Your way now climbs around this little ravine before, at a further ladder stile, entering an expanse of open woodland, grazed by sheep. To the left the river is now in a deep gorge, the surrounding rocks carved and polished smooth with the action of the water. This is Ghaistrills Strid, very much less fearful a place than the Strid at Bolton Abbey, but nonetheless to be treated with respect as the river courses through deep, fast flowing channels. The name "Ghaistrills" is a mystery but is thought to refer to the ghostly sound made by the water through the rapids.

Yet only a few metres further on as you follow the path round, the river is calm, broad and still, often whisky brown in colour above its pebbly bed, from the peaty moors and fellsides from where it drains. This is a good place for wildlife if there aren't too many visitors around with dogs, boats and stone-throwing children – dippers in the pools, swallows skimming the water, and if you're lucky perhaps even a kingfisher giving a vivid flash of brilliant colour as he darts across the banks.

Make your way carefully down the rocky path to the riverside and continue alongside the river to a stile and narrow pasture to re-enter the wood. The path now bears away from and above the steep sides of the river which here forms a series of deep dark pools known as Black Dubs – "dub" being local dialect for pools.

Keep in the same direction through a lovely area of scattered oak and birch wood, a good place to see the odd primrose or wood anemone in spring. As the wood thins away, bear right away from the river towards the gate and a step stile into Wood Lane. Go left into Wood Lane for about 100 metres before turning right at a stile and gate into Grass Wood Nature Reserve.

Please keep to the main path through this Reserve, owned and managed by Wharfedale Naturalists' Trust, to help reduce trampling and damage, for this is a woodland of national importance for its wildflowers. Among the more common to be seen in the late spring and early summer are primroses, cowslips, wood anemone, bluebell, bird's eye primrose, false oxlips, lily of the valley and several species or orchid. It goes without saying that it is illegal to pick wildflowers in the wood and care should be taken at all times to avoid leaving litter or doing anything that could remotely cause a fire. In addition to wild flowers, there are a wide variety of native trees including such lovely specimens as bird cherry, blackthorn, guelder rose, yew, hazel, Scots pine and many more, as well as plantations of larch, spruce and beech. Bird life is also particularly rich including nuthatch, willow warblers, finches and the occasional woodpecker.

The track climbs steadily uphill through the woodland. After about 200 metres there is a clear junction of tracks. Take the way-marked route to the right, still uphill. This is not the actual line of the public right-of-way as on the Ordnance Map but is easier to follow and Trust wardens prefer this path to be used. A steady uphill ascent now, but with fine views between the trees as you ascend. At the summit keep on the main path, avoiding crossing paths. You now begin to descend into a rocky, thickly wooded gorge.

Keep the same direction, through dense, dark woodland, following a clear, stony path until it levels out and you see ahead a green sign indicating the site of a prehistoric (Celtic) village – a settlement of the ancient Brigantes who occupied this part of Grass Wood and nearby village field settlements, probably well on into Roman times. These Roman British settlements pre-dated the present village of Grassington which, as its name implies, is an Anglian settlement probably near the ancient enclosures or "ings" created by the Brigantes.

You are directed round the edge of the prehistoric site until you reach a wall and steep stile, Park Stile, ahead. Cross. Your path is almost directly ahead but to the right of the wall and barn ahead.

Make for a field gate where the path enters a broad and usually muddy lane by a barn. As the lane bears right, look for a stile by steps in the wall corner – this climbs at the corner of a field.

Climb this field and keep the same direction towards the wall with a gap stile straight ahead. Go through here, making your way to the farm ahead, the path following a concrete track, almost always muddy, round the outside of the cow house and through the farm gate into Chapel Street, Grassington.

Continue along Chapel Street past Town Head, a beautiful 17th century yeoman farmer's house with stone mullioned windows. The cottages on the left as you walk further down Chapel Street are typical lead miners' cottages, and probably contained families of five or six in appalling overcrowded conditions during the height of the mines' prosperity in the early years of last century.

You arrive at Grassington Town Hall with its handsome clock. At the little Square there is a choice of ways back through the village. Perhaps rather than going down the Main Street on the right, take the stony track immediately down to the left of the cottages ahead – this leads to Pletts' Barn, a magnificent 18th century barn where John Wesley himself once preached. It is now a shop specialising in walking equipment and on the first floor is a small art gallery.

# Kettlewell and Starbotton

*This walk uses a lively stretch of the Dales Way and returns along an elevated limestone terrace with exceptional views of this steeply glaciated section of valley. Time required: 2-2½ hours.*

*Terrain: Paths and tracks by riverside and across pasture. Fairly level – but a number of stiles to cross.*

*Parking: In the National Park car park at Kettlewell.*

*Public Transport: Keighley & District service 71 from Skipton bus station via Grassington to Kettlewell; Service 800 (Dalesbus) at weekends April-October from Ilkley, Bradford and Leeds.*

*Refreshment: Kettlewell – choice of cafes and inns. Toilets in the village. Pub at Starbotton.*

*Map: OS Outdoor Leisure Sheet 30 (Yorkshire Dales North and Central); Stile Maps: The Dales Way Route Guide.*

FROM Kettlewell bridge take the path through the gateway at the far side of the bridge, soon bearing right with the signpost down to the riverside and a kissing gate. You will soon be walking along one of several sections of this path which have been stabilised by the National Park authority to counteract the erosive effect of the river and human feet.

This path, well-used, is easy to follow and clear on the ground, waymarked in places, as well as being clearly indicated by stiles and gates.

You go through a second kissing gate, the path veering away from the river, soon going along an enclosed, stony track past a large barn. Cross open fields, then back into an enclosed way. Ladder stiles and usually gates mark the way.

Notice how steep the valley sides are – a superb example of a U-shaped glaciated valley, the steep sides carved out by the great Wharfedale glacier in the last Ice Age. Note, too, the ridges in the field – these are "raines" or "lynchets", remnants of ancient terraced arable field. They were used from Anglian times until the early 19th century, mainly for growing oats, the staple fare of the Dales for many centuries. There are also some attractive areas of semi-natural woodland clinging to the steep slopes.

More ladder stiles and the path bears right close to a great bend in the river, which loops away and then is rejoined by the path as it loops back. This is another resurfaced section of path. Keep ahead

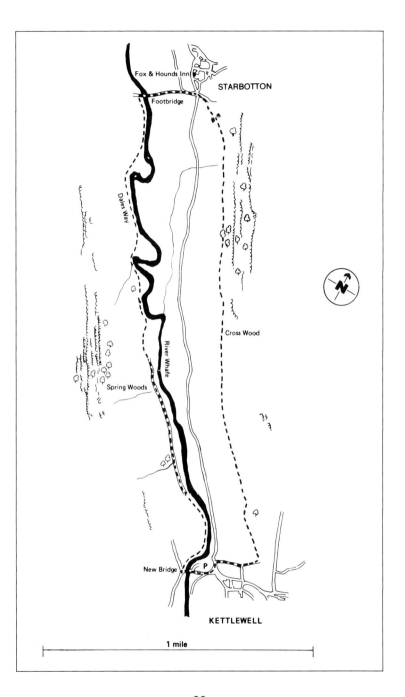

across a tiny footbridge, then over a field and a little complex of stiles to reach the footbridge across the River Wharfe and an enclosed, stony way which takes you into the edge of Starbotton.

The unusual name of this settlement probably means a stony valley but could also indicate a place where standards – poles – were cut. It is a village of attractive stone cottages and houses which date from the 17th century, but the 20th century examples, in local material and traditional style, blend well with the old – a tribute to the National Park planners.

If you seek refreshment, the Fox and Hounds Inn on the main road at the far end of the village is a typical small, stone-floored Dales pub, welcoming walkers. Otherwise cross the road, turning right and then first left where, below a drive from cottages, a path, signposted, bears right through a gate. Follow the green way through gateways. The path on the Ordnance Map is shown as going sharp left up the narrow pasture to the rickety gate above, but the path most walkers use and clearly the farmers prefer to be used, is through the next gate and behind the barn ahead where a gate rejoins the original path. Follow the wall along to a pedestrian gate in the wall corner.

This path is easier to follow, from now on clearly visible on the ground and indicated by ladder stiles throughout. You soon begin to ascend slightly, following a natural limestone terrace above narrow enclosures to the right, with increasingly fine views down and across the valley with river and road below you. The path goes along the edge of a wood, mainly beech and gnarled thorn clinging to the hillside. Follow the way as it curves round a shallow ravine, over a shallow beck, then finds its way back into open pasture. Step stiles over the many crossing walls mark the way. You pass another small wood, Cross Wood, the path now veering towards the wallside to your right, above the lower pastures with their scattered barns.

Soon Kettlewell comes into view, clustered below the great bluff of Middlesmoor Scars under which the main road to Skipton climbs. The path enters another little wood by a wooden step stile, then follows the wall round as it curves to the right, to go through a little stile and gate in to a narrow enclosure by houses.

You'll find yorself in Kettlewell's back lane – ahead to pubs, cafes and car park.

# Cray Gill and Hubberholme

*This classic walk at the head of Upper Wharfedale and into Langstrothdale offers some outstanding views and is rich in historical interest. Time required: 2-2½ hours.*

*Terrain: Paths and tracks across open pasture. One steady uphill section. Generally easy underfoot.*

*Parking: In the National Park car park at Buckden.*

*Public Transport: Keighley & District service 71 from Skipton bus station to Buckden via Grassington; Service 800 (Dalesbus) at weekends April-October from Ilkley, Bradford and Leeds.*

*Refreshment: Buckden – Buck Inn, cafe, shop. The White Lion at Cray and the George at Hubberholme are also on the route. Toilets in Buckden car park.*

*Map: OS Outdoor Leisure Sheet 30 (Yorkshire Dales Northern and Central); OS Pathfinder SE87/97. Stile Maps: The Dales Way Footpath Map.*

BUCKDEN, as its name implies, was once a foresters' settlement and hunting lodge in the royal hunting forest of Langstrothdale. The last village in Upper Wharfedale, it is situated under the flanks of Buckden Pike and makes an excellent starting and finishing point for a walk.

From the car park go through the gate at the top, closing it behind you, and walk along the green track which gradually ascends the hillside – Buckden Rakes. "Rakes" or "raikes" is a northern dialect word for a hill. This particular track is doubly interesting, almost certainly being on the line of Julius Agricola's campaigning road built to subjugate the warlike Celtic Brigante tribes in the first century and originally linking the fort at Ilkley (Olicana) with that at Bainbridge (Virosidium).

It is a well drained limestone track, soon going through a second gate and entering thin, mainly ash, woodland, Rakes Wood. It is a steady climb and you need to take your time, being rewarded by ever more specticular views across the top of the dale as you ascend.

Gradually you emerge from the wood and follow the track as it bears right, through a top gate. The path, less distinct now, levels off and follows the wall through more gates, the path to Buckden Pike soon bearing off right. Keep ahead towards the next gate by a stile but take the path signed to Cray, which leaves by a small pedestrian gate and bears down steep pasture. Take care here as

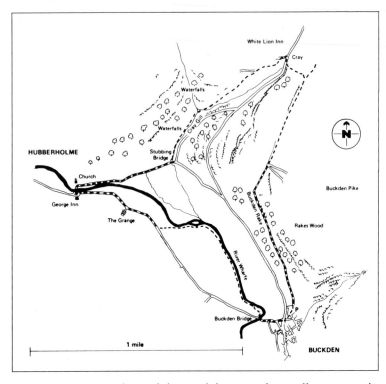

the way is steep as the path bears right towards a wall, to a gate in the bottom corner of the field. Ford the shallow stream (convenient stepping stones can easily be found) to emerge on the road immediately opposite the White Lion Inn at Cray.

The route continues along the farmtrack to the right of the inn, but almost immediately forking to a gate to the right and above the barn ahead, rejoining the farmtrack behind the farm. At the next barn and farm ahead take the narrow, enclosed way between stone walls to the left and below the farm (signed) which leads to a pedestrian gate.

The path is a faint green way which bears slightly right across soft turf above the shoulder of a shallow valley – Cray Hill – before descending.

This is quite a magical place – you are looking into a great green bowl set within the hills that look somehow grander and more spectacular than their height suggests. The intensely green hillside, rocks, scattered trees and tiny beck plunging over a series of cataracts are like a wild, Romantic painting – a Turner or Caspar Friedrich – made animate.

The way passes the largest of the shimmering waterfalls to a little stone packhorse bridge over Crook Gill, a side valley. Continue alongside the wooded ravine, over an almost hidden bridge of limestone slabs, to reach another stile before you finally join the lane at a gate and stile just west of Stubbing Bridge. Turn right to follow the lane to Hubberholme.

Hubberholme Church, dedicated to St. Michael and all Angels, dates from Norman times and is a fine example of a small dales church. It was probably a forest chapel in Langstrothdale, as Upper Wharfedale is still known beyond Buckden, and may have occupied a pagan Anglo-Viking burial site. It is built with local stone and roofed with lead from local mines. Its very remoteness probably saved its most remarkable feature, a richly ornamented rood loft, erected in 1558, which survived damage in Civil War times and is one of only two in Yorkshire. The ashes of the Bradford born playwright J.B. Priestley lie scattered in the vicinity – Hubberholme was, understandably, one of his favourite places in the Yorkshire Dales. A plaque in the church recalls his presence.

Also of interest is the George Inn which until relatively recently was owned by the church, being kept by the churchwarden until 1965. It is the scene of the annual "Hubberholme Parliament", a thousand year old tradition during which the vicar auctions the grazing of a 16 acre field, Kirk Pasture, the income so raised being used to help local pensioners.

From the George Inn, walk along the lane towards Buckden for about 400 metres. Go past Grange Farm, to where a gate on the left, a short distance past a barn, gives access to a footpath, part of the Dales Way, which follows a hedge to the riverside. This attractive path follows a long curve of the river embankment over stiles, to join the lane at a field gate. Turn left to Buckden Bridge and walk along the lane up to the village with its ancient green.

# Malhamdale

MALHAM is justifiably famous. Within a short area of the main village car park, in a triangle of countryside containing the village, the Cove, the Tarn and Gordale Scar, you've an area which is one of the showpieces of Europe, where complex faulting of the earth's structure has exposed the huge beds of pale Great Scar limestone, here weathered and eroded to produce a juxtaposition of scar, crag, ravine and polished limestone pavement that, in its visual splendour, is pure theatre. Little wonder the poets, painters, the diary-keepers, the topographers have come to Malham to pour out their hyperbole at terror-creating crags, at the sublime splendour of beetling cliffs. Add to this a rich human history, an archaeology which lies all around, and there's something worth seeing. You don't have to be an expert to know there's something very special about Malham.

But there are two quite distinct, and contradictory sides to Malhamdale. There's the head of the valley, that magic triangle, where everything is larger than life, on an epic scale. But turn the other way, follow the little River Aire downstream, and you find a quite different, gentle dale, a valley of soft colours and quiet pretentions, of subtlety, offering, time and again, views across to theatrical Malham that quite take the breath away, those gleaming, white crags seen through haze, something quite magical, romantic. Away from the busy paths are little known, even forgotten ways that need patience to nose out – even with the help of the National Park footpath signs and occasional waymarks.

# The Cove, Gordale and Janet's Foss

*Few short walks in the North of England offer such dramatic beauty and historic interest as this classic walk from Malham village which compresses so much in so short a distance. Time required: 2 hours.*

*Terrain: Stony paths, steep steps and several stiles.*

*Parking: National Park Centre car park, Malham.*

*Public Transport: Pennine Motors service 210 Skipton-Malham.*

*Refreshment: Choice of pubs and cafes in Malham.*

*Map: OS Outdoor Leisure Sheet 10 (Yorkshire Dales Southern Area). Stile Maps: Malhamdale Footpath Map.*

FROM the car park and National Park Centre turn left into the centre of the village, bearing right across the bridge past the Lister's Arms, taking the first narrow lane, left, which climbs past the Youth Hostel – named John Dower House after the author of the major report which led to the establishment of National Parks in England and Wales, and which was written in Malhamdale.

Keep ahead past the farm, through a gate, along a narrow, enclosed track. A second gate, slightly left (signposted), leads to a fieldpath by a wall, which soon leads to a ladder stile. The path through old field and by ancient walls, now descends to give spectacular views of Malham Cove. Keep ahead through a gap to the next stile, by a wall past the ruin of Bombey's barn, and ahead by remnants of walls direct to the Cove.

Malham Cove, a huge natural amphitheatre of rock, nearly 300 feet in height, was created by a gigantic prehistoric waterfall. Geological change has forced the stream underground, leaving a dry valley where the torrent once flowed, though history records exceptional floods when the waterfall flowed once again. This is Great Scar Limestone, here elevated by the action of the Craven Fault, the rock superbly exposed. Dark stains are the result of actions by mosses and lichen. Note the stream does not come, as many have supposed, from the Tarn, but from Smelt Mill Sinks, near the great chimney on Malham Moor.

Cross the stream, and return back through attractive boulder and scrubland to join the main path back towards the village, but turning up, sharply right, the well-signed path which ascends steps around the outside of the Cove. These steps were built by the National Park Warden service to combat serious erosion and make the route better for walkers and now blend into the landscape.

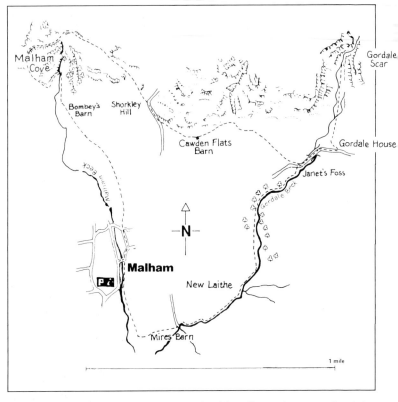

The path swings right to cross a double stile to the summit of the Cove – a wide extent of limestone paving. Take care crossing the polished clints and grykes, where harts-tongue fern and herb robert grow – an ankle can easily be twisted here. The views, from the pavement, are justifiably famous, looking down the whole of green Malhamdale, to Pendle Hill and Bowland beyond, a superb sense of space and aerial beauty.

Make your way carefully to the far side of the Cove, to cross another ladder stile by a gate leading to hillside pasture. Bear right, climbing uphill, across a long field, away from the Cove. At Tarn Road cross the lane by ladder stiles to a path which soon swings through the craggy pasture down to the wall below. Follow this left into Grey Gill, through a little sheep fold, continue to a kissing gate with steps on the right. You are on the far side of Cawden Hill – notice the strange lumps and mounds in the pasture, especially noticeable in late afternoon or winter sun. These are the outlines of ancient Iron Age fields and small enclosures. You are literally treading on history.

Cross to the next ladder stile, keep alongside the wall to the stile in Gordale Lane by Gordale Bridge. Turn left, soon reaching the little pedestrian gate and a clear, gravel path leading to Gordale Scar.

Gordale Scar is one of the wonders of England – a deep, scoured ravine, remnants of a shattered cavern, where the cliffs overhang and yew trees cling to the crags. At the head of the gorge a waterfall, white and foaming, tumbles after rain (miserable trickle after drought). It's an eerie, atmospheric place, best on a stormy day, in November, when you've the place to yourself. Little wonder poets, painters, diarists, travellers from all over England made a pilgrimage to Gordale as Romantic passion gripped England like a fever. Poet Thomas Gray 'shuddered' with delight, Wordsworth, Turner, Girtin, wondered; James Ward's great painting hangs on the walls of the Tate Gallery, London. You can see a study for it in Bradford's Cartwright Hall.

Though a right of way ascends the fragile tufa (limestone deposits) of the falls, to climb up it is like scrambling up the gargoyles of Westminster Abbey. View, enjoy, cherish, then retrace your steps. Treat the vulnerable screes that shoulder the Scar the same way.

Turn right into Gordale Lane, but soon after the bridge look for the little wicket gate, left, which leads to a slippery path down to Janet's Foss – the name a corruption of 'Gennett' a local fairy, foss a Norse word for waterfall. It's a perfect little fall, in a wooded glade, its apron of tufa a backcloth to the white spume of water as it falls into a still, circular pool.

An attractive path now heads through the woods – the clear path leaves the woods by stiles. Keep to the edge of the fields, by the stream, soon passing New Laithe, over twin stiles to cross a farm access track, on to reach Mires Barn to rejoin the Pennine Way. Turn right, through stiles until you reach the little footbridge that brings you back into the village centre.

# Pikedaw

*A walk rich in geological interest and industrial history, also offering spectacular views across the head of Malhamdale and to Malham Tarn. Time required: 2 hours.*

*Terrain: Stony tracks, steep moorland.*

*Parking: National Park Centre car park, Malham.*

*Public Transport: Pennine Motors service 210 Skipton-Malham.*

*Refreshment: Choice of pubs and cafes in Malham.*

*Map: OS Outdoor Leisure Sheet 10 (Yorkshire Dales Southern Area). Stile Maps: Malhamdale Footpath Map.*

FROM the National Park Centre car park turn left, along the stony, enclosed track which branches right, directly behind the car park, climbing uphill behind the village, with a fascinating view across the rooftops. Ignore the first track left, but take the second, near a house with a fine eighteenth century dovecote in its gables, to climb steeply uphill to a fork in the tracks. Take the left fork here, continuing to climb past a couple of fine traditional field barns, until the way plunges down across a beck, with a slab bridge for pedestrians. On the right is a gate and stile. Cross, soon crossing the little beck again, and continue to the barn ahead. The stile is at the far side of the barn. The path, across rough pasture, now ascends a shallow side valley which runs close to the major fault line of the great Mid-Craven Fault. Notice the distinct change of colour in the vegetation between the rusty reds of the acid sandstones and gritstones to the left of the beck, and the lighter, sweeter pastures to the right. Ascend to the next crossing wall with its ladder stile, keeping the same direction where you'll pass the entrance to an adit or horizontal drain, with the datestone 1876, a relic to the lead mines on Pikedaw.

Continue up to the next ladder stile on the top wall; cross, bearing right up the slope, through crazy outcrops of limestone and lime-stone pavement. Keep the same direction to join the Settle-Malham bridleroad, a tall signpost assisting the walker to find a bearing.

Left here, along the old green road, used by, among others, Dorothy and William Wordsworth on their visit to Malham in 1805. You'll soon pass a covered manhole – a shaft into the Calamine (Zinc) mines described so graphically by Dr. Raistrick in *Mines and Miners on Malham Moor*.

Continue to the gateway, turning right to reach Nappa Cross, an

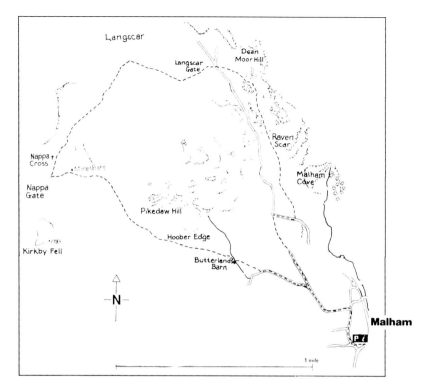

important Malhamdale monastic boundary and wayside cross set into the wall, which is also a thrilling viewpoint across the Cove and Scar, with Malham Tarn splendidly laid out in the foreground. The cross base is original, the shaft restored.

Follow the wall to where it bears right before cutting across to the gate ahead, through the corner of the next field, and across a third, keeping the same direction until the main Langscar Gate bridleway is joined, another ancient packhorseway, this time from Langscliffe in Ribblesdale. Turn right, through another gate, along the wallside to reach the Cove Road at a gate just above the cattle grid – Langscar Gate.

Cross the road directly, but bear right across the pasture opposite to a ladder stile, and path, parallel to the road, over a ruined wall and further ladder and step stiles to reach the Cove Road.

Turn left here, climbing uphill 100 metres or so to where the road bends sharp right. Go through the gate left along the bridleway which goes the length of a long field to enter an enclosed, stony track which leads down to Malham village. Paths will take you to the centre of the village; turn right to the car park.

# Weets Cross

*A walk offering glorious views across Malham village, Malhamdale and some of the most spectacular geological features. Time required: 2½ hours.*

*Terrain: Riverside paths, lanes and open moorland.*

*Parking: National Park Centre car park, Malham.*

*Public Transport: Pennine Motors service 210 Skipton-Malham.*

*Refreshment: Choice of pubs and cafes in Malham.*

*Map: OS Outdoor Leisure Sheet 10 (Yorkshire Dales Southern Area). Stile Maps: Malhamdale Footpath Map.*

FROM the National Park Centre turn left towards the village, but take the little footbridge, right, identified as the Pennine Way, which crosses Malham Beck. The path crosses a couple of stiles, a long field, another ladder stile and a junction of paths. Keep ahead to another stile across the field, crossing Gordale Beck at Black Hole, moving away from the riverside, over more stiles, climbing slightly with fine views across to Kirkby Malham and Hanlith. Soon after the ladder stile above the wood, the path swings into a large field. Your way, not immediately obvious, is left, uphill, to the top corner of the field, through a field gate and into a farm track.

You are soon at a junction of lanes. Turn sharp left, to leave the Pennine Way, to follow Windy Pike Lane. This is a gentle climb up towards Hanlith Moor, rewarded by magnificent panoramic views back across Malham village, the Cove, the line of the Mid-Craven Fault where limestone and sandstones meet, clearly visible, and the dramatic outcrops of limestone terraces and pavements which gleam in sunlight.

The walled track swings upwards, eventually leading through a gate onto Hanlith Moor, an expanse of yellow-brown moorland grass. Your way, indistinct on the ground, keeps the same north-easterly direction, soon indicated by helpful moorland marker posts. Keep the posts in sight (various Land Rover tracks can mislead) until you eventually reach a ladder stile, beyond which more clearly defined tracks lead up to the white triangulation station of Weets Top.

This is, in clear weather, a thrilling viewpoint, back across the huge expanse of Calton and Hanlith Moors across Malhamdale, to the east the clearly defined outlines of Sharp Haw and Thorpe Fell

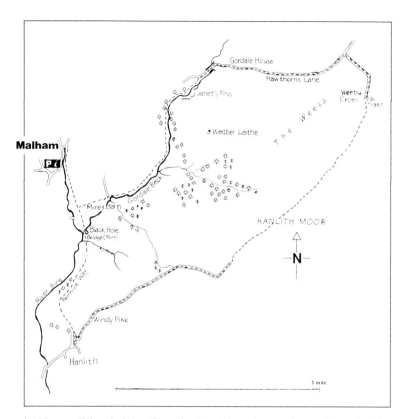

in Upper Wharfedale, Grassington Moor beyond; northwards into the while limestone scars of Gordale.

Immediately through the gate, left, is Weets Cross, a single column of stone in an ancient cross base. The cross marked the boundary of a number of old townships. The cross base is monastic in origin on an ancient crossroads of bridle tracks and packhorse-ways, placed by the monks of Fountains Abbey partly as a waymark, partly to consecrate the way, as crosses are placed in Alpine passes to the present day.

A short walled track from Weets Cross leads to Hawthorns Lane. Turn left down to Gordale Scar (see Walk 10) continuing to Gordale Bridge. The wicket gate left leads to Janet's Foss and the clearly marked path (described in Walk 10) back to Mires Barn and the Pennine Way to Malham.

# Malham Tarn

*This is another classic walk, this time utilising the Pennine Way between Malham village and the Tarn, returning along the spectacular Dry Valley – Watlowes – to the Cove. To make a full day's walk, of eleven miles, the route can be combined with Walk 14 to Darnbrook. Time required: 3 hours.*

*Terrain: Stony paths and moorland tracks.*

*Parking: National Park Centre car park, Malham.*

*Public Transport: Pennine Motors service 210 Skipton-Malham.*

*Refreshment: Choice of pubs and cafes in Malham.*

*Map: OS Outdoor Leisure Sheet 10 (Yorkshire Dales Southern Area). Stile Maps: Malhamdale Footpath Map.*

FROM the National Park Centre, turn into the village, keeping left at the junction in the village centre along the Cove Road, but looking for the little kissing gate which takes the Pennine Way through an attractive strip of woodland on the right. This re-emerges at a stile on the road. Follow the lane uphill, past the magnificent, much photographed seventeenth century farmhouse at Town Head, to reach the kissing gate, and the broad, well frequented path to the Cove.

Follow the Pennine Way towards the Cove, through kissing gates and over stiles, perhaps taking time to go right up to the base of the Cove (see Walk 10), otherwise branching left along the Pennine Way up steps, around the western side of the Cove, over the double stile to the limestone pavements and the spectacular view down Malhamdale, taking care over the well polished stones.

Once over the pavement, bear left over a ladder stile and along Trougate. This is an ancient manorial way, in use since Iron Age times, and if you look carefully as you walk, you will see traces of old Iron Age and monastic enclosures – a particularly fine one is to the right past the second ladder stile. This large expanse of pasture is still known as Prior Rakes, reference to the Canons of Bolton Priory who once owned it. At little pools where the paths fork, keep to the Pennine Way, right, as it crosses rough pasture to the tarmac road. Soon after you cross the road there is a stone base of a monastic wayside cross.

Keep ahead now, to enjoy increasingly lovely views of Malham Tarn, one of the very few natural lakes in the Yorkshire Dales, lying on a bed of impervious Silurian slates, which has been exposed

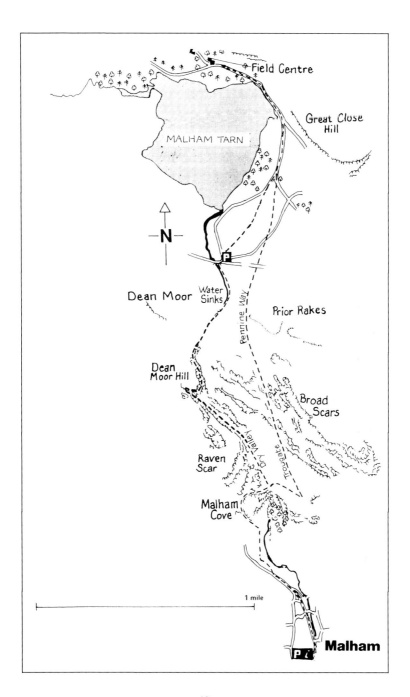

Field Centre

Great Close Hill

MALHAM TARN

N

Dean Moor

Water Sinks

Prior Rakes

Pennine Way

Dean Moor Hill

Broad Scars

Dry Valley

Trougate

Raven Scar

Malham Cove

1 mile

Malham

through the action of the North Craven Fault – a thick glacial moraine impounds the water.

The Tarn once supplied the monks of Fountains Abbey with fish. Tarn House, now a nationally famous Field Study Centre, was built by the Victorian philanthropist, Walter Morrison, to replace an earlier hunting lodge. Among eminent guests were John Ruskin and Charles Kingsley who wrote his popular polemical novel *Water Babies* as a result of his Malhamdale visit, describing the Tarn, the Cove and limestone terraces as part of the background of the book.

The Field Studies Centre provides an excellent introduction to the natural history of the area in the form of a *Nature Trail* leaflet which is usually on sale at a little honesty box dispenser at the entrance to the woods, or at Tarn House itself. Follow the path through the woods to the House, perhaps calling in to pick up a leaflet about the wide variety of special interest courses which are held through the year. Access is permitted on the main path through the estate, but do not trespass in the woods which form part of a carefully protected nature reserve.

Return to the estate entrance, this time bearing right along the attractive path which goes close to the Tarn edge, with delightful views across the water. This crosses to the road and car park.

Cross the bridge over Malham Water, taking the gate left to join the bridleway over Dean Moor, soon forking left across to the beck at Water Sinks, where Malham Water vanishes to reappear at Aire Head Springs (see Walk 15). Continue along the wallside below Water Sinks, soon entering a narrow ravine, the Dry Valley, scoured out by Malham Water before an easier underground passage was created. Look carefully for a narrow path, right, which contours carefully round a stile and joins the main path down the rocky, dry gorge of Watlowes.

Slow going along here – rough, ankle-twisting boulders, but you are walking through a miniature canyon surrounded by crags. Cross a ladder stile, and you'll soon find yourself at the Cove. Keep right across the limestone pavements to the ladder stile and well defined path back to Malham village.

# Darnbrook and Middlehouse

*A walk in the very heartland of the Yorkshire Dales – remote land-scape of desolate beauty and grandeur. This walk can be usefully combined with Walk 13 to make a full 11 mile ramble – the only sensible option for public transport users. Time required: 3 hours.*

*Terrain: Stony paths, steep steps and several stiles.*

*Parking: National Trust car park, Malham Tarn (Grid Ref: SD 894658).*

*Public Transport: Pennine Motors service 210 Skipton-Malham then follow Walk 13 (total of 11 miles).*

*Refreshment: Choice of pubs and cafes in Malham.*

*Map: OS Outdoor Leisure Sheet 10 (Yorkshire Dales Southern Area). Stile Maps: Malhamdale Footpath Map.*

FROM the car park follow the main track to the entrance to Tarn House estate, continuing along the estate track through and past the Field Centre, then along the main drive to the point where, at a stile right, the Pennine Way turns north. Cross the pasture to a gate, the Pennine Way now following along a shallow, dry valley, past a small barn, around a curve, across a stile. When the wall goes left the Pennine Way follows it down to a gate, then bears half right (avoid tractor tracks sharp right) uphill to join the road from Malham.

A mile's unavoidable road walking now, fortunately downhill and with a grassy verge to avoid traffic which can be busy on sunny afternoons – but until there's someone with wit and wisdom to create a footpath down Cowside Beck, there's no alternative. Fine views across to Fountains Fell, however, as you start the descent, with the Pennine Way snaking up to its bleak summit.

Darnbrook, though originally a monastic grange belonging to Fountains Abbey, is a modern farm, attempting to increase pro-duction from hill-farming with techniques that include some arable farming – an ambitious project in so remote an area. Just before the farm, a wicket gate gives access to a signposted path through a small plantation. Cross over the ladder stile. The next stile is to the left of the barn ahead. Descend and cross Cowside Beck at a footbridge.

The path now climbs murderously steeply up the fell – little sign of a path on the ground, but keep the same direction as you ascend heading, on a slight surve, roughly due south. You are soon aware

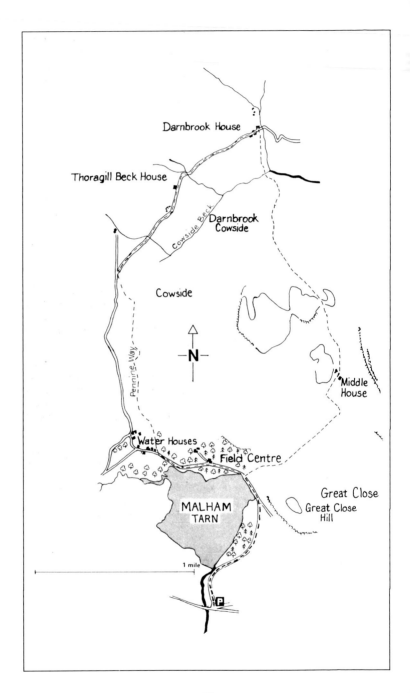

of an increasing grandeur in the landscape. A line of hummocks in the hillside in the fell emerge as an ancient, sunken wall, of incredible antiquity. Look across to Cowside, left, and Yew Coggar Scar with woods and waterfalls and back across Darnbrook fell. Another ladder stile in the crossing wall at the fell top marks the line of path. You are now in wild and open fell, with only the scattered yellow mountain pansy, in spring, to give contrasting colour. The path veers left, south-east. Head for a narrow 'saddle' or dip in the hills ahead, and if you are on course, a ladder stile in the next crossing wall is a valuable waymark.

Cross, keeping the same direction, heading towards a scatter of trees at Middle House. Cross to the farm, meeting the bridleway from Arncliffe – the Monk's Way. Middle House is described by Dr. Raistrick as a fine example of an outlying Norse farm settlement, the name derived from the 'meet low' or meeting place; a traditional Dales farmhouse, 360 years old, its predecessor mentioned in fourteenth century documents, but now sadly deserted, although preserved as a monument by the National Trust.

The path goes round the outside of the buildings at Middle House, following the wall around. Note the incredible complex pattern of medieval fields below the farm. Follow the wall round to the gate and stile, but leave the more obvious path to bear right down a steep dip across a wide pasture.

This great pasture, which extends across to the east, is known as Great Close and was in the eighteenth century the site of the Great Close Cattle Fair, where Scottish drivers brought as many as 5,000 cattle from the Highlands for sale to the English markets, as well as sheep and horses. An inn, now long vanished, existed near Great Close Scar.

Cross the fences ahead at a convenient stile, and roughly parallel with the telephone wires, climb the narrow saddle in the hills directly ahead. At the summit a sudden splendid view of Malham Tarn awaits. Descend the steep slope to the woods of the Field Centre entrance, turning left along the track to the estate gates. Bear right here to follow the path by the Tarn which leads directly to the car park.

If you're returning to Malham village for car or bus, take the path by Water Sinks and Dry Valley as described in Walk 13.

# Aire Head Springs and Acraplatts

*This short walk in the gentler side of Malhamdale uses less frequented ways and offers unusual, but memorable views, of the dalehead. Time required: 2 hours.*

*Terrain: Fieldpath and tracks.*

*Parking: National Park Centre car park, Malham.*

*Public Transport: Pennine Motors service 210 Skipton-Malham.*

*Refreshment: Choice of pubs and cafes in Malham; Victoria Inn at Kirkby Malham.*

*Map: OS Outdoor Leisure Sheet 10 (Yorkshire Dales Southern Area). Stile Maps: Malhamdale Footpath Map.*

FROM the National Park Centre turn left towards the village, but opposite the Methodist Chapel cross to the ladder stile which leads into a long field on the east side of Malham Beck. Keep ahead through fields along a fairly clear path, over two more ladder stiles and a little footbridge, towards Aire Head Springs – bear slightly right towards an ash tree above the Springs.

Aire Head Springs is a remarkable resurgence of the stream which flows from Malham Tarn, down Water Sinks on Dean Moor (see Walk 13) and through complex passages and fissures in the bed rock, actually passing underneath Malham Beck to form the source of the River Aire – the river so blackened and begrimed which flows through the city of Leeds. Here's the actual source, pumping from the ground like a great fountain.

Cross the stile, noting other resurgent springs, continuing to the next stile. The path now follows an attractive little limestone shelf – look back to enjoy splendid views of Gordale Scar and the Cove. This leads to a little enclosed way zig-zagging around the pretty mill goit at Kirkby Malham Mill (now a private house).

Immediately at the stile past the mill, leave the drive to take a faint, sloping path upwards, to the right, leading to a ladder stile. Cross this, looking for the faint way which goes between telephone posts to another ladder stile. Cross the next narrow field, but take the next ladder stile, left, at the field gate, leading to a short length of path generously granted by a Malhamdale farmer to keep walkers, especially the young, away from a dangerous road. At the gate cross this road directly to a track which ascends to the right, but after about 100 metres look for a stone step stile before the gateway, left.

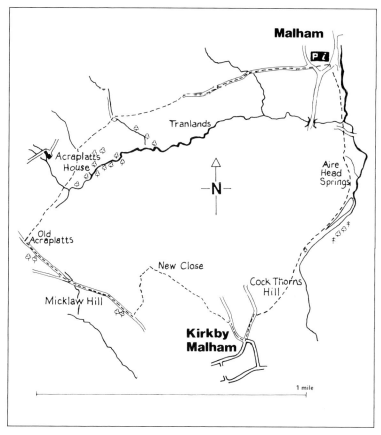

This leads to a lovely little field path, following the wall upwards to another stile in a crossing wall. The next ladder stile before the farm leads to the farm drive. Follow it left towards the Settle road, enjoying panoramic views from here across and down Malhamdale. Note the line of the Mid-Craven Fault across Gordale immediately opposite as far as Weets Top, across the valley, with the golden-brown acid vegetation contrasting with the pale green pastures where underlying limestones sweeten the soils.

Follow the lane uphill, over Micklelaw Hill, until a track forks off right. Take this, and about 100 metres beyond the cattle grid, just before a spinney, cross a ladder stile by a gate, left.

The path descends, again with quite splendid views back down across to Malham and the Cove. Make for the wooded gill ahead, heading to the left of a ruined barn below. Cross a step stile in the wall, and continue to cross the gill by a little footbridge. Your way now bears slightly left, below Acraplatts House Farm, to a ladder stile at the top of the wood ahead. Bear right now, towards Malham, with glorious views as you descend, over a series of ladder stiles, by a wall, finally entering an enclosed track which emerges directly at the National Park Centre.

# Calton Moor

*A ridge walk along which to enjoy superb views of both Wharfedale and Malhamdale, returning via the delightful Winterburn valley. Time required: 4 hours.*

*Terrain: Moorland and fieldpaths.*

*Parking: On quiet roadside verge in Calton village.*

*Public Transport: Pennine Motors service 210 Skipton-Malham as far as Airton Village Green then walk eastwards up the lane to Calton (half a mile).*

*Refreshment: None.*

*Map: OS Outdoor Leisure Sheet 10 (Yorkshire Dales Southern Area). Stile Maps: Malhamdale Footpath Map (part).*

CALTON earns a footnote in the history books by being the birth-place of Major-General John Lambert, the brilliant Cromwellian General, who was born at Calton Hall in 1619 – not in the present house, but a previous house on the site.

Follow the lane to the top of the village, bearing left at the junction which soon becomes a stony way across Foss Gill beck, towards a sheepfold.

A little care is required here. Avoid the temptation to walk into the Gill. The bridleway goes through a gate into the sheepfold, left, continuing not along the obvious Land Rover tracks left, but a fainter way directly ahead, which loops round slightly right, before becoming a more distinct way climbing steeply uphill. As you climb, bearing slightly right with the ravine below you, the curve of a wall will come into sight. Head for this wall corner, your path being about 100 metres to the right of this wall.

A steep, steady climb now, over rough moorland, with traces of the path visible as the wall approaches. A gate in the crossing wall marks the line of the path, which now swings away from the wallside to avoid a very boggy patch, returning to a point about 100 metres from the wallside.

You are now walking along a huge ridge, a great tongue of land with, in good conditions, clear views to either side. Soon the white triangulation post at Weets Top will come into sight as an ideal bearing point, though it takes a tantalising long time to reach.

If the day is clear there are magnificent views from here – west across to Pikedaw above Malham, with Ingleborough in the distance,

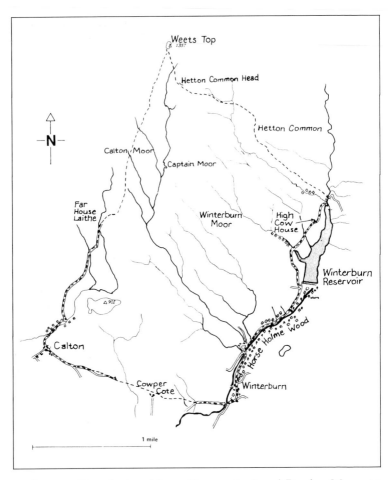

to the east Grassington Moor, Simons Seat and Barden Moor, to the south Pendle Hill, Longridge and the Fells of Bowland.

Your path is almost due south-eastwards, marked by a fellgate across from Weets. Make for this, descending and re-ascending across a dip. Once through the gate, follow the field wall down, but soon swinging left across and down the centre of a long field. You will notice a brighter green field, with a barn to the left. Next to it is a field of rough pasture, with a gate to its right-hand corner. Make for this, following a wall along to the next gate. Right again here, following the line of a ruined wall, through an old gateway right, crossing to the next gate. You are in a long narrow pasture descending to the bridge at the top of Winterburn Reservoir, a long, silent strip of water in an austere moorland setting. As you make your way sharp right (not across the bridge) fording Whetstone Gill, look for a little boundary stone on the right marked 'L & L Co.' – the Leeds and Liverpool Canal Company, for this reservoir was built to supply the thirsty locks of the Leeds-Liverpool Canal at Gargrave.

Through the gate, the track, green and attractive, climbs to High Cow House Farm. Pass around the outside of the farmhouse and along the main track to Way Gill Farm, either picking up the footpath past Way Gill, or continuing along the farm track past the reservoir cottage which soon becomes the main lane down the attractive wooded Winterburn valley.

Follow this lane through to the scattered hamlet of Winterburn, pausing to look at the little chapel, now a private house, in the fields just before the road junction. This little chapel was founded in the 1670s by Lady Lambert, daughter-in-law of General Lambert.

Keep ahead at the crossroads, turning right at the next junction to cross Winterburn Beck. Go 250 metres on the road, then right across a stile to a lively fieldpath which slopes up the pasture to a stile in the fence by old trees ahead. Cross, keeping ahead up the slope to Cowper Gate Farm. Go through the gate opposite the farm, then the gate at the farm, but right again around the outside of a small enclosure, climbing up to a gate up and beyond the farm.

Bear right here, descending to a stream, cross at a stile by ash trees, climbing to the barn, Farlands Laithe, ahead. Go through the gate to the left of the barn, then round to the far side of the barn. Keep ahead to pass in front of a ruined barn (Horselet's Laithe), through a gateway right, across to a stile. You'll find yourself now on a grassy way, soon becoming an enclosed way, muddy in places after wet weather, which soon emerges in Calton. Airton is half a mile away.

# Kirk Gait

*A walk to explore some beautiful and little known footpaths on the edge of Malhamdale. Time required: 3½ hours.*

*Terrain: Fieldpaths and tracks.*

*Parking: A quiet verge by Airton Village Green.*

*Public Transport: Pennine Motors service 210 Skipton-Malham to Airton.*

*Refreshment: Victoria Inn in Kirkby Malham.*

*Map: OS Outdoor Leisure Sheet 10 (Yorkshire Dales Southern Area). Stile Maps: Malhamdale Footpath Map (part).*

PARK in a quiet spot in Airton, avoiding the risk of obstruction. There is a quiet lay-by by the bridge which holds two or three cars.

Airton is a pleasant, unpretentious village, focused around a triangular village green which has a cottage planted in the centre – a remarkable example of eighteenth century encroachment. There is a fine old Quaker meeting house and as a sign of rural revival, a nationally known outdoor clothing manufacturers.

From the village green walk along the Skipton road southwards, turning right, just before the derestriction sign, up a grassy track which goes behind Airton's outlying houses. Turn left at the lane, but at a fork in the lane, directly ahead, bear right along an enclosed farm track and bridleway. Continue straight ahead past Kirk Syke Farm along which is now a sunken green lane – look for blue dots on the wall and the gates which denote a bridleway.

Go through a gate by an old quarry and tip, near Well Head springs, to cross an open field to the field gate directly opposite (waymarked). Follow the wallside now, to the next fieldgate, left, when a blue arrow indicates the right of way along the fence side towards a barn. Follow a track from here to Bell Busk.

According to the older writers, Bell Busk earned its name as the place where a bell was suspended from a 'conspicuous' bush and rung to warn travellers on the ancient Leeds-Kendal packhorse road that the road was in flood; more likely the 'busk' was the bush, sign of a small roadside tavern, though no evidence of its existence is known. The present village was built to serve a long vanished silk mill, and has more recent significance for its railway station (now a guest house) which intil the 1950s was the local station for Malham – albeit a four mile walk or drive away. The village post office and shop survive.

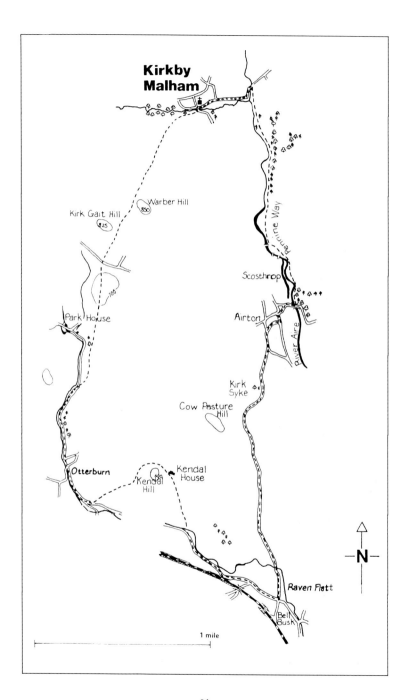

1 mile

Follow the lane, right for about half a mile. The next path leaves the road at a point when there are two field gates on the right and left-hand sides. The path, right, fords Otterburn Beck to cross the fence at the edge of the wood, through the gateway opposite and up the hill. (If the beck is too deep to be forded, a deviation may have to be made from the road bridge 200 metres west near Reek House Hill, keeping to field sides.) Follow the path through open pasture to Kendal House, a ruined farm, above left, cutting across by the summit of Kendal Hill, a typical glacial drumlin offering fine views across into the Ribble Valley, the name 'Kendal' linked to the old Kendal road below. Descend to the field gate below, to the left, crossing a field and footbridge to return to the road. Turn right into Otterburn.

A village mentioned in Domesday, and undoubtedly earning its name from that most delightful of British mammals (not entirely vanished from Craven), Otterburn surrounds both banks of the river. At the cross roads go directly ahead on what appears to be a lane, but soon becomes a beckside track, going up a lonely highland valley.

This is Kirk Gait, the old parishioners' way from Otterburn to Kirkby Malham church. At a gate into a little wooded ravine, the path, signposted, goes through the gate on the right, climbing onto a vestigal track across the shoulder of the wooded hill ahead. Follow this above the wood to another gate, again to enjoy some fine views, this time across Scosthrop Moor to the hills above Settle, the distinctive shape of Rye Loaf hill being a notable landmark.

Descend to a ladder stile ahead in the wall on the right – do not cross, but look for the step stile directly ahead. Keep ahead now to Scosthrop Lane and cross the ladder stile and the stile and gate to continue to Kirk Gait Hill, with, on the right, a most impressive lime kiln. The path now swings slightly left to the left-hand side of the wood up Warbler Hill, to a stone step stile, then descends, with impressive views, along the wallside to a pretty stone-arch footbridge. A slight climb now, across the centre of the field; aim for the wood ahead to locate a ladder stile. Follow the woodside to the next ladder stile, with superb views now across Kirkby Malham church and village, swinging right to another stile, leading to a wicket gate and slab footbridge across the ravine below the church.

Take time to see Kirkby Malham's beautiful church – removing muddy boots. The ancient parish church of Malhamdale, existing on an Anglian site, dates back from Tudor times, but mysterious Celtic-style heads built into the walls hint at its earlier origin. A contribution to the church's upkeep is always welcome. In the churchyard look for a curious grave where husband and wife lie buried at either side of a rushing spring.

The village, which boasts an inn, the *Victoria*, keeps its timeless charm. Go down to the crossroads beyond the bridge, turning left to Hanlith Bridge, at the far side of which the Pennine Way will return you to Airton. Keep to the riverside, looking for the stile, left, after about half a mile, which leads to further stiles across the footbridge, left. Keep ahead to Airton Bridge, turn right into the village.

# Eshton Moor, Winterburn Reservoir and Friar's Head

*This walk is an extension and adaptation of an old favourite, taking in the first four miles of the Pennine Way in Malhamdale, and returning via little used paths around Winterburn Reservoir, Friar's Head and Eshton Park; superb views throughout. Time required: 5-6 hours.*

*Terrain: Fieldpaths and tracks.*

*Parking: Public car park, West Street, Gargrave.*

*Public Transport: Pennine Motors service 210 Skipton-Malham or 580 Skipton-Settle services to Gargrave; Ribble 279 Skipton-Lancaster service to Gargrave. Regional Railways: Leeds Skipton-Lancaster line to Gargrave.*

*Refreshment: Choice of pubs and cafes in Gargrave.*

*Map: OS Outdoor Leisure Sheet 10 (Yorkshire Dales Southern Area).*

FROM the main cross roads on the A65 cross to West Street alongside the cafe. Keep along West Street to cross the canal bridge, keeping straight ahead where the lane bends right, along a stony track signed 'Unsuitable for Motors'. The new Gargrave by-pass will intersect the route at this point – go under the by-pass and follow the old lane in the same direction. Keep on past Gargrave House and up Heber Hill, soon giving good views of the rolling green hillocks or drumlins, formed from glacial waste.

After just over half a mile look for the stone stile, right, which takes the Pennine Way across open pasture, making for a gateway, left, uphill. Keep up the hill to the next gateway (look for way-marks), keeping to the left of a small plantation, before going through a gate on the right and crossing to a further gate near the summit of Horrows Hill – magnificent views along Malhamdale from here. Left along the wall now through further gates and gaps, bearing right alongside a wall, through a narrow enclosed section, descending to a narrow way between wall and road. A footbridge, left, takes the Pennine Way across the infant River Aire. Keep to the right-hand side of the wood, between wood and river, to the stiles leading onto Newfield Bridge.

Cross the bridge over the river, continuing along the Pennine Way by the riverside. This is easy walking through attractive

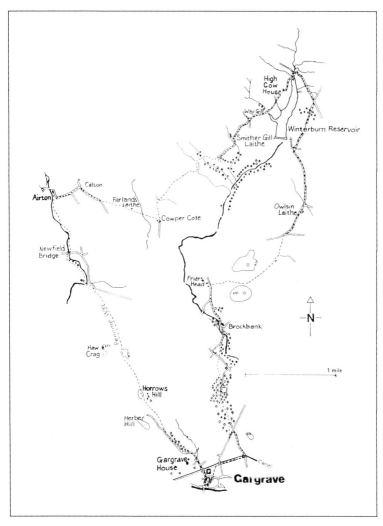

parkland, by Newfield Laithe, crossing pasture before returning to the riverside at Airton.

Follow the lane, right, uphill to Calton, keeping ahead when the main Winterburn road bends right, into Calton village, but turning right at the top of the village along the track which soon becomes a sunken, often muddy way, through gates. Keep ahead as the track peters out alongside tumbled walls, through a gap, then a stile, bearing right round a barn, Farlands Laithe. The path now descends a little ravine, crosses a stream by an ash tree and ascends to a farm, Cowper Gate. Go through the gate to the left of the farm.

Do not go through the farm buildings, but turn left. The path now veers uphill and climbs a low knoll before descending to cross a stream, bearing right to a gate in the fence. The path follows now an ancient, moss and grass-covered wall, perhaps the remnants of a medieval enclosure, bearing right, through a second gate, descending to a beck and further gate. Turn left here towards the barn, Windros Laithe, uphill. The path now veers right, through more gates uphill, into a wood, but going through a gate on the right. Cross the pasture, bearing left to the thin plantation of wood on the left, to another gate. Ahead now, looking for the gate which leads into the long drive to Smither Gill Laithe farmhouse. Follow the track, left, around the edge of the field by Smither Gill, turning right towards the isolated farmhouse at Way Gill. Turn right through the gate immediately at the farm, and descend to locate a stile in the far left-hand corner of the field below. This leads to the track round Winterburn Reservoir to High Cow House Farm. Go right behind this farm to find the gate which opens to a sunken green way to the head of Winterburn Reservoir, a supply reservoir for the Leeds-Liverpool Canal, and now an attractive bird sanctuary.

Go over the stone bridge at the head of the reservoir, following tracks uphill, but soon hairpinning back to climb the steep, rough pasture, making for the gate in the wall above. This is a crossing point of tracks (public transport users might consider keeping directly ahead towards Hetton to pick up the Dalesbus 71). To return to Gargrave go through the gate, right, heading across the moor to gates and an obvious gap in the plantation ahead – a little marshy so care is needed in the wood. Ahead, keep the same direction across the wall to locate gates in the wall corner above the reservoir dam. In the next big pasture, the way swings left, uphill, over a hillock. At the summit make for Owslin Laithe below, right. The path crosses a beck and goes through a gate alongside a barn and wall to emerge on the Hetton-Winterburn road.

Cross directly ahead on the bridleway by the wall which climbs yet another hillock by Scarnber Laithe to a shallow gap between the hills, through a gate. The next gate is in the field corner below right, descending a steep slope past mysterious prehistoric 'Pillow mounds' – probably Bronze Age graves – to Friar's Head. Turn left along the lane to enjoy this superb late Elizabethan house, with splendid gables and mullioned windows, one of the finest houses of its period in the Yorkshire Dales. It was built by Stephen Proctor, perhaps better known as the builder of Fountains Hall, which was constructed from the stone of Fountains Abbey in 1610.

Follow the lane, but where it swings right, take the track left, which climbs by gates and stiles to another 17th century farmhouse, Brockabank. Follow the path in front of the house, going along the farm drive and down over the river, but look for the stile, left, that takes the path directly across a paddock to the lane east of Eshton Grange.

Cross, taking the path directly ahead to a stile, before veering left to another stile in the corner of the wood that forms part of Eshton Park. Keep right through the wood, following the path alongside the fence until it emerges in parkland. Cross the park, to a stile in the fence below, keeping ahead to where the path joins the lane below the cross roads. Turn left for a few yards, before going right along the lane to Ray Bridge on the Leeds-Liverpool canal. Now take the canal towpath pleasantly into Gargrave, past historic warehouses and wharfs where calamine (zinc ore) from Malham Moor was, in the late 18th and 19th centuries, loaded onto waiting barges.

Just past the canal locks, a kissing gate leads to a ginnel (alleyway) into the centre of Gargrave for cafes, car parks, buses and trains.

# The Three Peaks
# and Upper Ribblesdale

THOSE three magnificent mountains of Yorkshire, Ingleborough, Whernside and Penyghent, hold a special affection in the hearts not only of Yorkshire people but of people throughout England. The popularity of the mountains, and in particular the Three Peaks Walk, one of the most popular challenge walks in the country, has inevitably caused serious problems. Paths are so eroded in certain sections because of the passage of so many thousands of boots, that deep, unsightly scars now blight the noble peaks, and evil quagmires have destroyed the pleasure of the walk. Remedial work through the National Park's Three Peaks Project has restored many of the worst sections, but much remains to be done.

The aim of this book is to suggest some of the many alternatives available in this splendid area of the Yorkshire Dales. By any standards, it is a superb landscape, on a grand, heroic scale; whenever you are within the area, those great summits, enormous shapes, remain huge, brooding presences. But in much of the area, many of the paths are little known and neglected, including Ribblesdale itself, a dale grossly underrated by people who pass the Helwith and Horton quarries and dismiss the valley as not worth exploration.

Inevitably, walks to the summit of the three great mountains are included. No one can pretend to know the area who hasn't enjoyed the thrill of an ascent of Penyghent, Ingleborough or Whernside. So classic routes to each summit are part of this book.

But the main aim of this book is to disperse the pressures away from the crowded summits on to quieter ways, not to see them also over-used – there is no likelihood of this happening – but to emphasise that there are riches unimaginable to explore away from the dreary trail of bobbing anoraks along the main Three Peaks Walk. Marathon walks can become a mistake, an ecological disaster, young people dragged round miles of fine mountain landscape sponsored for a cause, however worthy, that does not relate to the area and its unique beauty. Farmers and landowners suffer damage, nuisance; the delicate ecology of the area is disturbed, destroyed; the landscape suffers.

So better to spread the load, seek alternatives that offer opportunities to enjoy a landscape of rare quality that deserves to be enjoyed, savoured, lingered over.

It's the geology that makes the Three Peaks so very special – the peaks themselves, gigantic layer cakes of gritstones, shales, Yoredale limestones, and the massive Great Scar limestones, pocked by shakeholes and potholes, riven with limestone scars and gills of often indescribable delicacy of beauty, enjoying a rich and rare flora – much of the Three Peaks area is an Area of Special Scientific Interest or Nature Reserve. It's a landscape which can only be discovered on foot, and offers riches at any season of the year.

# Victoria Cave

*Victoria Cave, one of the most remarkable archaeological sites in Northern England, is only one of the many highlights of a walk which over a very short distance gives a real taste of some of the Craven's most spectacular limestone scenery. Time required: 2 hours.*

*Terrain: Stony paths and tracks, steep in places.*

*Parking: There are three large and well-signed car parks close to the centre of Settle.*

*Public Transport: Leeds-Settle-Carlisle line to Settle; Pennine Motors Bus service 580 Skipton-Settle; Ribble 279 Skipton-Lancaster service.*

*Refreshment: Choice of pubs and cafes in Settle.*

*Map: OS Outdoor Leisure Sheet 2 (Yorkshire Dales Western Area).*

SETTLE is an excellent centre for rambling, strategically situated on the edge of the limestone escarpments of Upper Ribblesdale. A pleasant, comfortable market town, the "capital" of the Three Peaks country, it has excellent shops and a wide range of cafes and pubs, and even outdoor shops if you've arrived without the necessary gear. Find time to visit the Museum of North Craven Life open most summer weekends.

From the Market Square follow Constitution Hill from the north-eastern corner of the Square past the Co-op, climbing steeply past cottages and 18th century houses. Soon beyond the edge of town, take the right hand fork along a stony track, enclosed, climbing past woods to a gate. Keep ahead alongside the wall, along the track which, though fainter, remains easy to follow. This once formed part of the monastic packhorse track to Langcliffe used by the monks of Fountains Abbey who had extensive lands and sheepwalks in the Settle and Malham areas. It was part of a network of tracks and packhorseways which were developed between outlying granges and farms and the parent Abbey, and included the famous Mastiles Lane, between Ribblesdale, Malhamdale and Wharfedale.

The way continues through three more gates. As you see a small wood, above right, bear towards this wood towards a small gate below the wood. Continue to the gate at the right hand corner of the next field behind the wood, Clay Pot Plantations. Turn right up the metalled track, through a gate and climbing towards the limestone scars. Soon past a small barn, right, the track bears left, climbing up towards Langcliffe Scar. A line of low crags ahead and

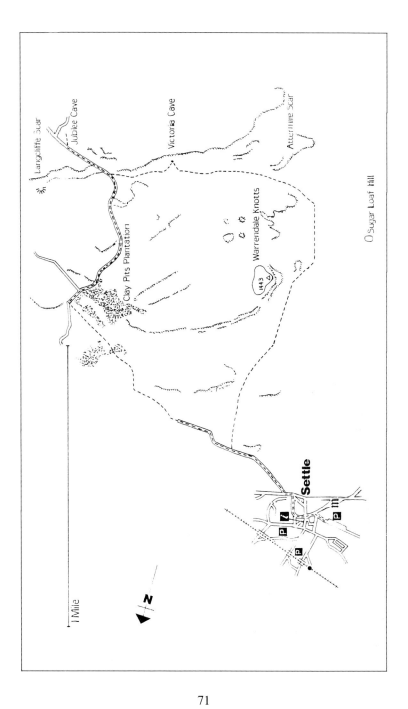

right contains the little Jubilee Caves; take time to explore the fascinating formations, where significant archaeological remains have been discovered.

Retrace your steps to the stile, right, and follow the path along the wallside. As you approach the line of a ruined wall on the right, a faint track left climbs up rocky scree to the wide entrance of Victoria Cave. Discovered by accident in 1837, the year of Queen Victoria's accession, this was initially little more than a crevice, before being opened out in the 1870s by archaeologists of the Victoria Cave Exploration Committee under the direction of the British Association for the Advancement of Science. Discoveries included remains of spotted hyaenas, hippopotamii, elephants, deer, bears and rhinoceros in the layers of glacial deposit and cave debris, and evidence of prehistoric and Roman-British human occupation over a long period. Some of the finds are to be seen in the excellent Museum of North Craven Life in Chapel Street, Settle. Take care when in the cave to cause minimum disturbance or damage to cave walls and floor surface; on no account leave litter.

The views from both Jubilee and Victoria Cave are magnificent, over the limestone crags and edges into Ribblesdale and beyond to Bowland. The area behind this section of Langcliffe Scar, including Settle Bank, forms the only official open access area in Ribblesdale. See the OS map for boundary details. Descend on the path that bears left down to the main path along the wall, across a stile, following the wall through a shallow limestone valley; continue to descend past the dramatic shoulder of Attermire, left, with Warrendale Knotts, the startling formations on the right.

These formations, like miniature Dolomite peaks, have a fascination and a splendour that totally belie their modest height particularly if caught in the afternoon sun, forming classic "karst" limestone features. After the gate, turn right following the wall to the stile below, crossing a former rifle range. Cross the stile, continue to a gap in the wall ahead, before bearing right to the wall corner, following the wall to a gate and stile ahead. The path now descends, steeply, across pasture. The rooftops of Settle are suddenly in view, the path dropping steeply, before bearing left to rejoin the main Langcliffe track to Settle.

# Cleatop Wood

*This short walk offers panoramic views across Ribblesdale and Bowland from little used footpaths south of Settle; a walk to discover the delights of little known Cleatop Wood. Time required: 2 hours.*

*Terrain: Stony paths and tracks, steep in places.*

*Parking: There are three large and well-signed car parks close to the centre of Settle.*

*Public Transport: Leeds-Settle-Carlisle line to Settle; Pennine Motors Bus service 580 Skipton-Settle; Ribble 279 Skipton-Lancaster service.*

*Refreshment: Choice of pubs and cafes in Settle.*

*Map: OS Outdoor Leisure Sheet 2 (Yorkshire Dales Western Area).*

FROM the rear of Settle Market Place go past the Midland and Trustee Banks, along the High Street towards the Folly, but keeping ahead along Chapel Square to Greenfoot Car Park (a convenient place to leave a car if doing this walk). Cross the car park to the main exit, past Greenfoot bungalows, into Ingfield Lane. Go left here, but as the lane swings left, turn right into a gravelly track, signposted to Mear Beck. This track soon becomes a stream with a causeway, and unusual footbridge. Continue as it winds past the inexplicably named Fish Copy Barn, climbing narrowly above a shallow ravine to join a farmtrack at Hayman Laithe.

The way is directly ahead, over a wooden stile, to the stone step stile in the field beyond. Cross to the next stile, keeping alongside the wall, left, then up to the corner of the wood where another stile will be found. Keep below the wood, with a gap in the field corner, right. Continue by the wall below the wood, descending to cross a beck and ravine to the next stile. Climb up and through the scattered woodland directly ahead, looking for a small pedestrian gate in the wall, left, immediately above Mearbeck House.

Cross to a green track marked by wheel marks, turning left through a gate. This track winds uphill towards Cleatop Wood. As the track comes close to the wood by a stream, look for the ladder stile, left, leading into the wood. Cross, turning sharp right behind the wall, when a faint path will be discernible with an attractive little waterfall to the left. Follow the path to a wooden footbridge, and by carefully fashioned steps climb up to a junction with a track. Turn right; the path, faint at first, soon becomes a delightful green way through birch and pine Cleatop Wood, of mixed pine, larch, oak, birch, and beech, is owned by the Yorkshire Dales National

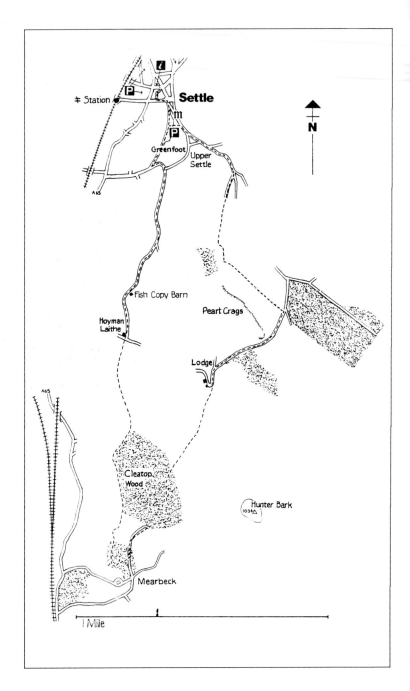

Station

**Settle**

Greenfoot
Upper
Settle

A 65

Fish Copy Barn

Hoyman
Laithe

Peart Crags

Lodge

A 65

Cleatop
Wood

Hunter Bark
1034△

Mearbeck

1 Mile

N

Park Committee as a woodland conservation area, and is rich in botanic interest. Please keep to the footpath through the wood.

At the woodtop are quite breathtaking views across Settle town and the dominant Giggleswick Scar; beyond a splendid panorama of the Bowland Fells and the green pastures of Ribblesdale; the familiar shape of Ingleborough and the limestone scars of Ribblesdale. Penyghent is to the north. Bear right at the summit with the path which leaves the wood at a gap stile. Your way is directly ahead and down to Lodge Farm below. Keep to the right of the farmhouse alongside the wall to the gate; this is a lovely open pasture with splendid views as you descend.

Beyond the gate a track turns right, soon reaching a junction of tracks. Bear right to a ladder stile by a gate, above. The track climbs past rhododendrons and pines, and the picturesque craggy ridge of Peart Craggs. At the next gate, by open land traversed by the metalled road over Hunter's Bark, turn back sharp left through the next gate into the field, left. Follow the field wall downhill, through a gap right above a wood. As you cross the brow of the hill, the whole of Settle town and its twin village of Giggleswick are spread before you, with Giggleswick School's green-domed chapel as a prominent landmark. Both townships, with their backcloth of limestone scars and fells, have an incomparably lovely setting.

Continue downhill to locate a stile in the bottom right hand corner of the field, below the wood. Turn right, below the field wall descending to join a short stretch of enclosed way to a gate, along the top side of the next wall to to a further gate leading into Mitchell Lane. Turn left in the lane, descending to meet the Airton road in Upper Settle. Directly ahead is the town centre.

# Feizor and Smearsett

*A walk by the magnificent limestone ridges of Upper Ribblesdale, with two strange monuments, one of ancient hillfarms, the other of Victorian industry. Time required: 3½ hours.*

*Terrain: Stony paths and tracks, steep in places.*

*Parking: There are three large and well-signed car parks close to the centre of Settle.*

*Public Transport: Leeds-Settle-Carlisle line to Settle; Pennine Motors Bus service 580 Skipton-Settle; Ribble 279 Skipton-Lancaster service.*

*Refreshment: Choice of pubs and cafes in Settle; pub and shop in Stainforth.*

*Map: OS Outdoor Leisure Sheet 2 (Yorkshire Dales Western Area).*

FROM Settle Market Place, cross to Kirkgate, almost opposite the Town Hall, but before reaching the Victoria Hall, turn sharp right, after Dugdale's shop, down a narrow ginnel by the tall columns of a high brick viaduct carrying the Settle-Carlisle Railway. Continue past the top car and coach park to join the main A65. Keep left to Settle Bridge over the river, crossing to pick up the footpath, signed, in an enclosed way around the edge of the playing fields. Follow this path around to a stile; cross a small field to the next stile and along a high embankment, with the river below; an attractive, lightly wooded pathway. Cross the next field to the Stackhouse Lane. Immediately across the lane a further stile and wicket gate leads to the path along the inside of the wall by the lane.

The path, at a gate, bears left around the outside of an estate wall, through scattered woodland. At the telegraph poles (signpost nearby) turn sharp left, climbing steeply uphill. Ahead is an ash tree growing out of an outcrop; keep left. Directly beyond a ladder stile marks the line of the footpath, and a gate and stile continues the line of path, now along a faint green trackway. To compensate for the climb splendid views unfold behind, across the narrow valley to Fountains Fell and Penyghent, a rich, green panorama with a dramatic skyline.

Follow the track zig-zagging up, around the outside of field walls, before keeping to the right fork, through a gateway. After 50 metres or so on the left a low, stone mound is an Iron Age Tumulus, a burial site and moving relic of ancient civilisation. A complete skeleton was discovered buried here in the last century.

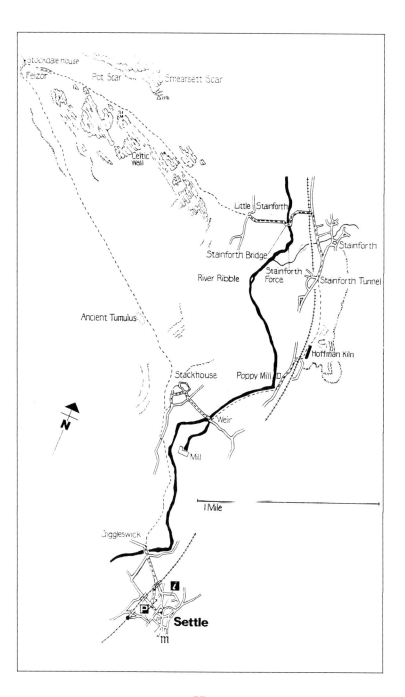

Stockdale house
Feizor
Pot Scar
Smearsett Scar
△1191

Celtic
Wall

Little Stainforth

Stainforth

Stainforth Bridge

River Ribble

Stainforth
Force

Stainforth Tunnel

Ancient Tumulus

Hoffman Kiln

Stackhouse

Poppy Mill

N

Weir

Mill

1 Mile

Giggleswick

*i*

P

**Settle**

m

Return to the track, which follows the drystone wall on the right. It soon crosses this wall at a gate and goes sharp left through a second gate, keeping the same direction, now across rough pasture, a pleasant carpet of green sward, easy on the feet and offering fine views across to Austwick, Wharfe Wood and, beyond, the distinctive flat-topped shape of Ingleborough itself. Another gate by a sheepfold, and the path soon descends across the pasture, worn bald to limestone pavement, descending easily into Feizor itself.

Feizor, one of the prettiest and least accessible of Dales settlements, remains quite unspoiled, but unless you have time to explore its charms (no facilities), turn right, by the ford, and immediately past a bungalow, through the gate right. You are now on an ancient monastic packhorseway between Lancaster and York (Feizor was a monastic grange), and you will soon be aware of a deep, sunken way to the right, at first carrying a streamlet, then the footpath, gradually ascending.

Cross a wall at a ladder stile, then along the way carved into the limestone, an obvious pass through the shallow gorge. To the left is the spectacular outcrop of Pot Scar, leading along the ridge to cave-studded Smearsett Scar, a dome of limestone capped by a triangulation post. The path descends. At the next stile, above small enclosures, leave the path ascending 200 metres uphill to the right at 45°; just above the skyline the end of a mysterious "Celtic" wall will appear – stretches of wall of rough, weathered limestone clint, some 20 metres long, 1½ metres high, ancient and weathered in appearance, covered with lichen. The origin of the wall is unknown, but is almost certain at least medieval in date, possibly part of a larger enclosure. Why only one stretch and a tantalising fragment remain is a mystery.

Retrace your steps. The path bears left to a ladder stile. Cross, keeping in the same direction along the grassy path uphill, to cross a stile and to enjoy another fine view into Ribblesdale across Stainforth. Descend easily via gate and stile to Little Stainforth. Follow the lane in front of the 17th century Stainforth Hall and camp sites to the splendid packhorse bridge and waterfall below, a lovely wooded stretch of the Ribble.

Continue to the main road. Stainforth is a most attractive village; the route continues by the path commencing just above the Youth Hostel on the main Settle road, below the by-pass. Go through a stile to a gateway opposite, and stile beyond, all below the huge form of Stainforth Scar. The path now veers right, towards the railway, curving around a gravelly way, crosses a further stile to reach, over a rickety bridge, Langcliffe's great Hoffman Kiln, a huge circular kiln, now unique in Britain, built in 1875. Over 400 feet long and 90 feet in breadth, its huge arches are reminiscent of the cellarium of Foundations Abbey in splendour. An explanatory note and diagram is to be found in the Quarry Office window. It is hoped the building will be conserved as a major industrial monument. The building now belongs to Craven District Council and entry is strictly by permission and at own risk.

Go past the kiln, through the quarry yard, but turn right behind the buildings to locate a level crossing over the railway. Cross with care. Walk past John Robert's paper mill, one of the last working mills in the Dales, to reach a path right, clearly marked by ladder stiles leading to Langcliffe Weir, with its celebrated salmon leap. Cross the footbridge, and go along the lane to Stackhouse, following the track directly opposite before going left at the letterbox, and left at the next junction to the lane corner. Just beyond Stackhouse, steps, right, lead to the footpath back, parallel to the lane and to the riverside path, to retrace your steps to Settle Bridge.

# Stainforth and Catrigg Force

*A walk to include one of the most famous packhorse bridges in the Dales, and perhaps the area's most delicately beautiful waterfall. Time required: 3 hours.*

*Terrain: Stony field paths and tracks, steep in places.*

*Parking: There are three large and well-signed car parks close to the centre of Settle.*

*Public Transport: Leeds-Settle-Carlisle line to Settle; Pennine Motors Bus service 580 Skipton-Settle; Ribble 279 Skipton-Lancaster service.*

*Refreshment: Choice of pubs and cafes in Settle; pub and shops in both Giggleswick and Stainforth.*

*Map: OS Outdoor Leisure Sheet 2 (Yorkshire Dales Western Area).*

BEGIN from Settle Market Place, crossing to walk down Kirkgate, at the side of Moore's shop, continuing past the car park, the Victoria Hall and under the railway arch, keeping directly ahead at the road junction. As this road bends right, keep straight ahead along a track behind terraced houses and by workshops. This leads to a paper mill and warehouse – keep to the track, swinging right, past the mill yard. This leads to the river, and a new footbridge. This is Giggleswick Memorial Bridge, erected in 1982 by the people of Giggleswick, as an inspired way of turning War Memorial funds into a valuable asset for the living – a short cut between the parishes of Giggleswick and Settle.

As you cross the bridge, look at the great rock, right, in the riverbed known as Queen's Rock. Go left along the riverside, but almost immediately fork right along a short ginnel; turn right at the road which leads into the centre of Giggleswick. This most charming of Dales townships, usually bypassed by tourists on the A65, is worth taking time over – houses and cottages of the 17th and 18th centuries, a beck along the main street, a fine medieval church. Walk by the beck until you reach Giggleswick School, that celebrated Dales public school. Branch left, uphill, with a splendid view of the famous School Chapel. Continue past the cricket ground, looking for a step stile and signpost on the right. Cross the field to the little circular building – the School Observatory.

Descend the slope, zig-zagging down to avoid the worst of the gradient, to the field corner, left, to a stile and a footbridge. Cross to the lane. Turn left, along the lane, past the golf course (site of the former Giggleswick Tarn, drained last century). At the main road

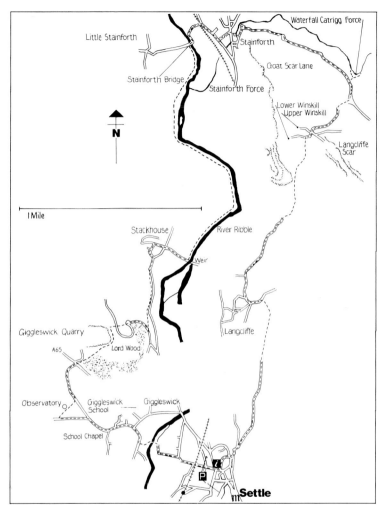

cross to the quarry entrance. At the right hand side of the quarry road (look for signposts), a footpath ascends the side of the quarry – if in difficulty you can join the path at the first bend in the quarry road. The path goes through a tall metal gate, steeply climbing by the quarry, with the huge, deep face of the Great Scar limestones, amongst the purest in Britain, hence their commercial importance.

At the top of the Scar, superb views – up Ribblesdale, across to Penyghent's massive form and back across the green, craggy pastures of Craven to Bowland. Descend the zig-zagging track down to the gate by the wood. Follow the track down to the wood back towards Settle. Now look carefully for a narrow gap stile on the left, covered by a little wooden lamb-gate, before the end of the track. Go through, on to a field path, cutting back along the fields, clearly marked by narrow stiles. This path is soon paralleled by the road, following the inside of a wall by the road, to a gate and stile at the enclosed woodland by Stackhouse.

Cross into the lane, immediately turning left along the track into Stackhouse, going first right at the next junction and right again to the lane. Cross the lane going straight down to Langcliffe Weir. Do not cross the footbridge; the stile left, leads to the riverside path. This path, easy to follow over a series of well marked stiles, follows one of the most delightful stretches of the Ribble – along the edge of Willy Wood, past Langcliffe Mill at the far side of the river before Stainforth Caravan Site comes into view. To the right a fine romantic gorge, waterfall and, to crown the effect, the elegant and ancient packhorse bridge, carrying the old way from Feizor to Ribblesdale.

Follow the lane uphill to the main road. Turn right towards Stainforth village, turning left past the c hurch to the village centre. Stainforth, once a grange of Selby Abbey, is a handsome village, now spared the roaring quarry traffic. At the lane corner, look for the stepping stones across the beck. Cross, then turn left up the steep, stony lane – Goat Scar Lane. At the top, a stile leads to a path which divided going right to the top of the fall, and left down the steps to the woods, to the bottom of Catrigg Foss, a tall slender column of water in a deep, narrow ferny gorge, spectacular at any time of year, but especially on winter days of hard frost when the spray turns to white gossamer.

Return to the stile on Goat Scar Lane. Go ahead to the gates, bearing left on the open pasture towards the stile and gate, left. Through here, along the lane towards Winskill, keeping ahead, through gates across the lane, towards Lower Winskill, birthplace of the fine Craven dialect poet Tom Twistleton, author of *Splinters Struck of Winskill Rock* published in 1867.

A stile, left, takes you off the track, descending to the field corner. The path descends through the wood, round the rear of the quarry. Look for a faint green way incised into the pasture, directly ahead, soon becoming a walled lane leading into the centre of Langcliffe, another delightful village with a fine green and fountain. Turn left up the lane climbing up the Malham road. As the lane bends left above the village, look for the field gate, right. Follow the wall, right, to the next gate. Keep to the wall, climbing, following above a wood, through gates, soon finding yourself on a distinct green track that becomes an enclosed stony track leading down into Settle's Constitution Hill.

# Penyghent

*Few mountains evoke greater feelings of affection among the fell-walking fraternity than Penyghent, its characteristic sphinx-like shape always a challenge and inspiration, its evocative Celtic name a reminder of the long history of man's occupation of the Dales. Time required: 3¹/₂ hours.*

*Terrain: Stony paths and tracks, extremely steep in places.*

*Parking: Large National Park car park in the centre of Horton.*

*Public Transport: Leeds-Settle-Carlisle line to Horton in Ribblesdale; Whaites or Ingfield Northern Rose 805 bus Settle-Horton.*

*Refreshment: Choice of pubs and cafes in Horton.*

*Map: OS Outdoor Leisure Sheet 2 (Yorkshire Dales Western Area).*

HORTON, an old Dales village, keeps its charm notwithstanding nearby quarries and related traffic. It's also a justifiably famous centre for walkers, given the accessibility of Penyghent and Ingleborough. Both the *Golden Lion* and the *Crown Hotel* as well as the *Penyghent Cafe* welcome ramblers, the latter offering an excellent range of light meals and mugs of welcome tea at almost any time of day; there's also a small well supplied shop with maps and outdoor equipment and guides. The village also has a useful shop at the post office, and a convenient camp site.

Though modest in height, Penyghent always remains a worthy challenge, and this classic route from Horton makes the best of the peak's special drama. From Horton car park walk back through the main part of the village, but just before the church look for the little gate, left, leading to a wall side path to the lane behind the church. Dedicated to St. Oswald, the church is, incidentally, well worth a visit, with much Norman and Perpendicular work. Left in the lane, but soon across the footbridge, right, and continue along the lane, past the primary school towards Brackenbottom.

The path for Penyghent is clearly signposted, immediately before Brackenbottom Farm, through a gate and straight ahead to a second gate and along the top side of a wall. This is a busy, well trodden path, soon climbing steeply to a stile, with frequent outcroppings of limestone. Not far past the next gate, crags of limestone require a little scramble; it is this Great Scar limestone that is so highly prized by the quarries disfiguring the valley above Horton immediately opposite. But as you climb you cross softer, acid shales and peat, sudden changes of terrain, until you reach the higher bands

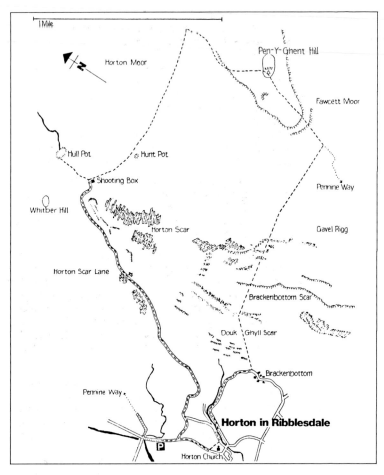

of Yoredale limestones near the summit. As you climb past the next stile, the dramatic form of Penyghent begins to loom before you, brilliant in clear light, a strange, almost menacing shape in cloud or mist.

At the top of the ridge, a ladder stile leads you on to the Pennine Way, with views, on a clear day, across to Fountains Fell. Left here, ascending the path that begins to wind murderously steeply across the great gritstone nose of the mountain, soon zig-zagging across a crag and boulder field (people sometimes suffer vertigo here). Hands are sometimes needed if it's wet or icy; a real sense of mountain climbing. At last, after a back-aching stretch, you are on the summit plateau, a smooth, peaty expanse, with a path curving gently up to the summit; a relief after the crags, but still a slog.

Except on the rarest days of still, calm blue skies, Penyghent is always a wild place, with a wind that threatens to tear the shirt from your back. Ahead the summit cairn and reassurance of the white trig. station, and a wall to shelter behind (which side will depend on the wind direction) for a well earned rest. Do not add to the desecration of the summit with orange peel or can rings. If it is one of those special clear days, the sense of space and air will be unforgettable – to the east the huge line of the formidable Fountains Fell, and the wild valley which is to form Littondale curving round out of sight; to the north-west, over the stile, Whernside and the rolling Ribblesdale drumlins; to the west Ingleborough, and south-wards, down Ribblesdale across to the rolling hills of Bowland.

The descent starts easily enough – directly ahead down a stony way before swinging right along a superbly engineered old miners' path, offering lively high level, panoramic views and a gentle descent, and relief, on many days, from the bitingly cold winds of the summit. You may even begin to feel warm again.

Your path now swings left, steeply down what appears to be the remains of a battlefield, but it is the effect of thousands of feet eroding the soft peak on the Three Peaks Walk. Various remedial works undertaken to restore the path by the Three Peaks Project will be evident. Follow the approved route to avoid further erosion, descending steeply to a peaty stream, and over a wall and stile. Not far past the stile look for a narrow path branching off left. This leads to Hunt Pot, a fine pothole, with a dramatic entrance. Keep away from the dangerous edge.

Return to the main path, through the little kissing gate to the old shooting hut. Now turn right here along the path for a couple of hundred metres or so until you reach Hull Pot, a chasm on a very much larger scale (on the surface) than Hunt Pot, and giving a thrilling impression of a great shattered cavern. You can walk round this great pot, looking at the little waterfall that on some days is a mere seep, but on those wet days when no views are available on the tops a fine, white foaming torrent In really bad weather the water cascades over the top along the dry stream bed. It is possible to scramble down into the main floor of the pot, but only do so with great care – modern boot soles slip easily on wet limestone.

Make you way back to the shooting hut. Through the gate on to Horton Scar Lane, easy walking after your early exertions, with fine views offering a profile of the conquered peak, and across the dry valley to your immediate left, with its splendid limestone formations. As you descend to Horton, patches of woodland soften the landscape and those last few hundred metres, past Douk Ghyll on your left (where the stream from Hull Pot remerges to form Horton Beck that you crossed at the start of the walk), offer a worthy conclusion to a walk which never fails to thrill.

# Alum Pot

*Alum Pot, one of the most awesome of Craven's many potholes, is the focal point of this fine walk which takes in some high level paths along Ribblesdale's limestone escarpments. Time required: 3¹/₂ hours.*

*Terrain: Stony paths and tracks, extremely steep in places.*

*Parking: Large National Park car park in the centre of Horton.*

*Public Transport: Leeds-Settle-Carlisle line to Horton in Ribblesdale; Whaites or Ingfield Northern Rose 805 bus Settle-Horton.*

*Refreshment: Choice of pubs and cafes in Horton.*

*Map: OS Outdoor Leisure Sheet 2 (Yorkshire Dales Western Area).*

FROM Horton's main car park, cross the river by the footbridge at the northern end. Follow the main road, keep ahead along the footpath to the right of the station drive entrance, up to Horton station, served on summer weekends by Dales Rail trains. Cross the line, carefully, through the gate behind, and along the main Three Peaks route, over the stile, and bearing right across pasture, dipping down before climbing steadily, then over the ladder stile by Beecroft Hall Farm. The path is clear and well defined through stile and gate. The huge expanse of Beecroft Quarry – ICI Horton – with its kilns, lies to the left.

But your path, climbing steeply now, crosses another ladder stile before climbing a narrow groove in the limestone – the celebrated Sulber Nick, and Iron Age track, possibly partially artificially made, to the great summit of Ingleborough. Follow it steeply up until you reach a wide, open plateau, at last reaching a cross-roads where a green Land Rover track crosses at right angles; this is Clapham Lane (see Walk 29), the old road from Clapham to Selside.

Turn right, following the track over the top of the plateau, spectacular views on all sides, Ingleborough summit looming above and to the left Penyghent across the green space of the valley, right. The way descends through a gate and across rough pasture above South House Farm. At the next gate, keep ahead as the track bears right, to the gate ahead, bearing slightly right across pasture to the gate and enclosed track ahead.

To visit Alum Pot, you must pay a small toll at the farm cottage at Selside, passed later in the walk. Go through the gate in the wall on the right where the path leads along a shallow valley to the huge, open caves of Alum Pot; with the swirling mists and

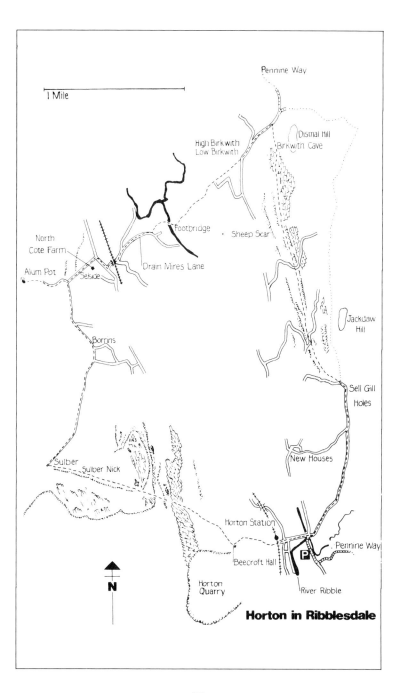

1 Mile

Pennine Way

High Birkwith
Low Birkwith

Dismal Hill
Birkwith Cave

North
Cote Farm

Footbridge

Sheep Scar

Alum Pot

Selside

Drain Mires Lane

Jackdaw
Hill

Borrins

Sell Gill
Holes

Sulber

1143

Sulber Nick

New Houses

Horton Station

Pennine Way

N

Beecroft Hall

P

Horton
Quarry

River Ribble

**Horton in Ribblesdale**

87

foams of the thundering torrent, little wonder that early travellers, quoting Virgil and Milton, thought it an extrance to Hell. The first descent was made, at considerable risk, in 1847. There are few more impressive sights in the Dales. But take care – the waterfall descends a sheer two hundred feet to a shelf with a further hundred foot drop. Above Alum Pot are the entrances to Diccan and Long Churn; fascinating insights into the strange and extraordinary underground world of the Dales. But do not enter except with a properly experienced and well equipped guide.

Return to the lane down to Selside, turning right on the main road into this little hamlet. Take the track, left (payment for visiting Alum Pot should be made at the cottage on the left), under the Settle-Carlisle line, keeping straight on at the first junction, and the right fork at the second, along the well named Drain Mire Lane, to a ladder stile, crossing wet land to a stile and footbridge across the Ribble. The path follows the beck across stiles, by Low Birkwith Farm. Keep to the left of the farm to pick up the path climbing up Copy Gill, across more stiles and through a copse to the lane at High Birkwith.

Follow the track, left, up across open pasture, bearing right at the top through a gateway above the little gill surrounding Birkwith Cave. You now follow a fine, high level route. Keep straight ahead below crags, right, to locate a stile near the wall corner. The path is parallel to the wall to the next stile, then bearing slightly left through a gap in the next wall, keeping ahead along a pleasant limestone shelf with attractive views, through gates, eventually bearing right to a stile behind a small building and the track the Pennine Way – at Sell Gill, close to Sell Gill Pot, an interesting fissure.

Turn left down Harber Scar Lane – easy walking, descending pleasantly to emerge at Horton's *Crown Inn*. Cross the bridge and up the hill to the railway station.

# Foredale, Wharfe and Moughton Scar

*This walk encompasses some of Ribblesdale's most dramatic land-scape contrasts – riverside and verdant valley, the raw and awesomely impressive quarry faces of Ribblesdale's modern industry, and quiet, austere mountain landscapes into remote and lovely Crummackdale. Time required: 4¹/₂ hours.*

*Terrain: Stony paths and moorland tracks.*

*Parking: Large National Park car park in the centre of Horton.*

*Public Transport: Leeds-Settle-Carlisle line to Horton in Ribblesdale; Whaites Coaches or Ingfield Northern Rose 805 bus Settle-Horton.*

*Refreshment: Choice of pubs and cafes in Horton.*

*Map: OS Outdoor Leisure Sheet 2 (Yorkshire Dales Western Area).*

FROM Horton's car park, cross northwards over the pedestrian bridge over the river. At the far end of the bridge, go left through the gap stile and down steps to the riverside. Follow the riverside path through the little gate behind the farm to the step stile. The path keeps to the river over a metal ladder stile. You soon pass a small sewage works; look for a clapper bridge right leading to a wooden ladder stile. Keep to the riverside, now entering an attractive wood, curving round.

Keep inside the wall at Crag Hill Farm, going over the stile behind the farm, then over the stile right leading round the back of the farmhouse, joining the farmtrack. Directly ahead is a barn; above and to the right of this a stile leads into a big field. On the right is a pedestrian gate and level crossing over the Settle-Carlisle Railway. Cross with care.

Ignore the stile, right, but keep ahead in the big field to find a stile in the far wall. Cross, now bearing slightly right, towards a large faded notice warning you not to proceed if the warning buzzer is sounding. Assuming it isn't, ascend past crags, with Arcow Quarry before you, and to the right dramatic exposures of ancient Ordovician slate strata in the quarry face. These ancient, hard rocks are in great demand for road surfacing, and the Ribblesdale quarries are major suppliers; for anyone interested in geology, the exposed quarry faces are fascinating features.

The right of way has been diverted from this point; even recent maps are still inaccurate. Ignore the inviting stile directly ahead, but turn left, downhill to a barn. Behind the barn is a ladder stile and a signpost. Cross through fields, often rather waterlogged,

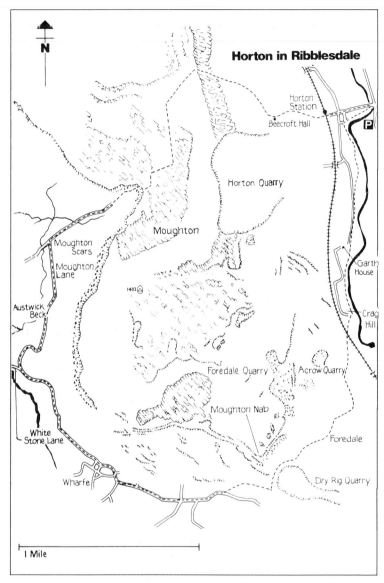

N

Horton in Ribblesdale

Horton Station

Beecroft Hall

P

Horton Quarry

Moughton

Moughton Scars

Garth House

Moughton Lane

1402

Crag Hill

Austwick Beck

Foredale Quarry    Acrow Quarry

Moughton Nab

White Stone Lane

Foredale

Wharfe

Dry Rig Quarry

1 Mile

crossing a drain by a bridge. Keep ahead to another ladder stile by a decrepit over-bridge. This leads to an old quarry railway track. Follow this right, towards the main Arcow Quarry road, keeping right along the road, but taking the fork, left, towards Foredale Farm and away from the main quarry entrance.

Go left along the tarmac track past the farm buildings at Foredale. Keep ahead, but as the track hairpins back climbing to Foredale Cottage, keep ahead through a field gate. Another quarry, Dry Rigg, lies ahead, biting deep into the ancient slates below Moughton Scar. Keep on the grassy track to the next gate, where a signpost will indicate the line of path around the outside of the quarry; at the time of writing a steep climb round the perimeter. Again, this is a path not offering conventional aspects of Dales beauty, but of interest to anyone wanting to learn more of Dales geology and industry. From the summit of the path there are fine views across to Wharfe Wood, over the curious dry valley separating the more familiar Carboniferous limestones and the dark slates of the Foredale area.

The path descends to a landscape of more tranquil beauty, through stiles, to the lane beyond Newfield House. Follow the lane for half a mile towards Austwick, past Far End House and White House; when the road bends, turn right along a road marked "Private – footpath and bridleway only" into the charming hamlet of Wharfe with its ancient cottages and primeval stillness. At a fork, go right through the gate in front of a while cottage (note the date and initials IWM 1726) on to a delightful green path, soon linking into a narrow enclosed way from lower Wharfe. This is White Stone Lane, a splendid packhorse way.

At a junction, leading down to a ford with little clapper bridges, take the right fork along Moughton Lane. This branch of the packhorse way winds splendidly into the heart of Crummackdale – a little known valley, mercifully inaccessible by car, with dramatic limestone escarpments forming a splendid natural arena. The track swings right, climbing steadily, and then steeply up the escarpment. At the summit, pause, to enjoy fine views behind. Avoid going to the right or the left on the cairned path at the top; your route is straight ahead, directly over a spectacular stretch of limestone pavement. Note the low green shrubs growing out of the limestone. These are junipers, rare survivors of the Dales' ancient tree cover.

A ladder stile in the wall ahead marks your path. Cross, going sharp left, alongside the wall, soon reaching and crossing a ladder stile, and bearing right (signposted) across rough pasture. Look carefully to see where a green, well-used track comes in from the left – the Three Peaks route from the summit of Ingleborough. Follow this as it curves right, swinging downhill towards Beecroft Hall. The path, clear and used by many thousands of feet, curves round across green pasture, over a stile, swings over a hillock, over further stiles, down across the railway line level crossing to the railway station. Ahead, Horton in Ribblesdale. Bear right across the footbridge over the river to the car park.

# Whernside

*This ascent of Whernside is very much preferable to the more familiar direct path up the scree slope from Winterscales, giving a true impression of the grandeur of the Dales' highest peak and the fine Whernside ridge. Time required: 3½ hours.*

*Terrain: Stony paths and tracks – some steep ascending and descending.*

*Parking: Roadside parking near the crossroads at Ribblehead.*

*Public Transport: Leeds-Settle-Carlisle line to Ribblehead.*

*Refreshment: Station Inn at Ribblehead; a small tea van is usually parked by the crossroads. The Hill Inn at Chapel-le-Dale, close to the route, also welcomes walkers.*

*Map: OS Outdoor Leisure Sheet 2 (Yorkshire Dales Western Area).*

RIBBLEHEAD, at the junction of the Ingleton-Hawes and Settle-Hawes roads, dominated by the famous viaduct on the Settle-Carlisle line, is the obvious starting point for an ascent of Whernside. The *Station Inn* offers a full range of facilities at the normal times, whilst many ramblers have had reason to be grateful for the little van usually serving hot bacon sandwiches in the worst weather, parked near the road junction. The recently reopened northbound platform at Ribblehead station now makes the area easily accessible by regular train services on the spectacular Settle-Carlisle railway.

Start from the *Station Inn*, following the track alongside the famous Ribblehead Viaduct. This impressive structure, with 24 massive arches, the highest of them 105 feet high, was built between 1870 and 1874. Time and the Pennine weather have taken their toll; massive repairs are required to the viaduct at the time of writing, threatening the future of the entire Settle-Carlisle line, England's most dramatically scenic railway.

As the track winds underneath the great viaduct, keep straight ahead alongside the arches to pick up the line of a footpath along the viaduct, alongside the embankment. You will see evidence of old spoil tips, part of the legendary Batty Moss encampment where armies of navvies lived during the building of the viaduct and near Blea Moor Tunnel in the early 1870s, with tragic loss of life. Many are buried in Chapel-le-Dale churchyard (see Walk 31).

Ahead the sidings, signal box and deserted signal box house of Blea Moor sidings. The track fords a beck, veers a little way from the railway, descends to ford more streams and swings left over

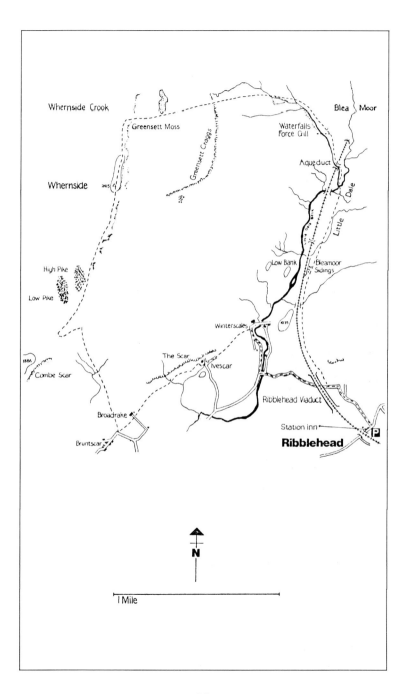

Whernside Crook

Greensett Moss

Greensett Craggs

Blea Moor

Waterfalls
Force Gill

Aqueduct

Whernside

2415

Little Dale

High Pike

Low Bank

Bleamoor
Sidings

Low Pike

Winterscales

1035

The Scar

Ivescar

1884

Combe Scar

Broadrake

Ribblehead Viaduct

Station inn

Bruntscar

**Ribblehead**

N

1 Mile

a magnificent viaduct that carries Force Gill Beck over the Settle-Carlisle railway. Cross, follow the path upstream, but keep ahead to the beck to Force Gill waterfall, a spectacular little Pennine gill, forming in the spring, a natural hanging garden of primroses and moorland grass.

Your route continues from Force Gill back to the path above the wall; leave the Craven Way path, climbing steeply up the hillside by wall and fence, up to the top of Coal Gill and above Greensett Crags, making for the high summit ridge, with Greensett Tarn to the right. This is a fierce climb, but compensated by spectacular views back down to Ribblehead and across to Park Fell and Ingleborough. Follow the path, left, along the summit ridge to the white triangulation station.

There is no logical reason why Whernside at 2,415 feet (796 metres), the highest of the Three Peaks, should be the least popular. It is a thrilling ridge, with panoramic views westwards to Gregareth, the Howgills and the Lakeland peaks, east and south to Cam Fell, Ingleborough, Penyghent, and southwards to the rolling hills of Bowland. No doubt the Three Peaks walkers seeing Whernside merely as a summit to "bagged" are to blame; it is, indeed, a mountain to be savoured, enjoyed, not rushed.

Descend the obvious, well worn path south-westwards (ignoring the scree track, left, which forms the Three Peaks ascent) across stiles and down what appear as gigantic steps as the gritstone cap yields to hard Yoredale limestones interspersed with shales, continuing down to High Pike and Low Pike. Turn left by a cairn to a stile, soon descending steeply down rough pasture, to a gateway, right, and gap to a junction of paths just north of Bruntscar Farm.

Ignore the main Three Peaks path ahead, unless you are heading for the *Hill Inn*. Turn left by a pleasant track, through gates, past Broadacre, and below the low, limestone scar to Ivescar and Winterscales, turning right along the metalled track from Winterscales by Gunnersfleet, bearing left to the viaduct and Ribblehead.

# Three Bridges

*This short walk, through the austere and treeless landscape near the source of the Ribble, offers exquisite beauty in remote gills, and three splendid little bridges, two of them man-made. Time required: 3 hours.*

*Terrain: Moorland paths and tracks.*

*Parking: Roadside parking near the crossroads at Ribblehead.*

*Public Transport: Leeds-Settle-Carlisle line to Ribblehead.*

*Refreshment: Station Inn at Ribblehead; a small tea van is usually parked by the crossroads.*

*Map: OS Outdoor Leisure Sheet 2 (Yorkshire Dales Western Area).*

FROM Ribblehead station walk for just over half a mile along the main Hawes road (grassy verge available), ignoring the first two signed paths on the right. Take the next through a gate on the right, and follow the wall to a second gate, before continuing along the wallside.

Thorns Gill is soon reached beyond the next gate, a quite hidden Pennine gill of incredible beauty, a deep limestone gorge, over-hung by rowan and thorn, the water-carved limestone forming sculptured shapes above and around the peat-brown stream. Across the gill is Thorns Gill Bridge, perhaps the finest of the Dales pack-horse bridges dating from the early 17th century, carrying the Craven Way on an ancient road from Settle to Dent. Almost certainly, the bridge served as a wet weather alternative to the Cam/Gearstones ford to the north.

Cross the bridge carefully. Climb the field above the bridge, littered with glacial erratic boulders, bearing left up to the left hand corner of the field. Keep ahead towards the trees and buildings ahead, the hamlet of Thorns. In living memory Thorns was a thriving hamlet, with several families, and regular social events including dances that attracted people from miles around. The deserted farmhouse and derelict cottages are a sad indication of economic and social change in the higher Dales.

The path continues through a gate on the right by a barn, signed to Nether Lodge and with the Ribble Way logo. Follow the wall uphill – one of the drumlins or mounds of glacial waste that give Ribblesdale such a sculptured appearance. Keep ahead through a stile and descend to a barn. The path goes around the barn and

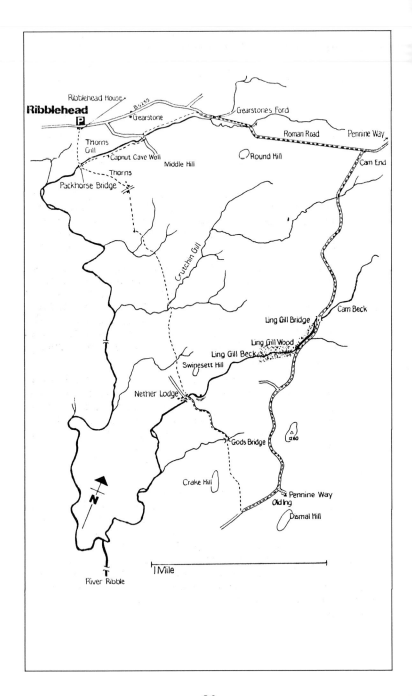

through a stile at the far side, heading left across rough grazing before bearing right to a stile in the wall corner.

You must now cross rough pasture and Crutchin Gill, bearing slightly right to the stile in the wall above; keep ahead to Nether Lodge Farm directly ahead. Through the gate on the farm drive, cross the stile almost immediately left, veering away from the wall up rough pasture to God's Bridge, on Brow Gill. God's Bridge, a huge slab of limestone, is one of many such natural bridges to be found in the Pennines, and again forms a fascinating little area, with a shallow gill and beck carving its way through the limestone gulley.

Through a gate, the path follows the wall towards High Birkwith. As you intersect the track, turn left towards Old Ing before joining the Pennine Way coming from Horton. Left along the enclosed way, now, past Calf Holes, and along the old coach road, ascending steadily to Ling Gill, a steep wooded gorge of great romantic beauty.

Ling Gill Bridge, at the head of the Gill, is in origin perhaps even older than Thorns Gill, dating from the 16th century. In the parapet is a plaque, now barely decipherable, which records how the bridge was restored "At the charge of the whole West Riding" in 1765. You now climb along a track which ascends bleak moorland to the summit of Cam Fell; at the summit of Cam End Cairn, the views back across to the Three Peaks with the Ribblehead viaduct, a noted landmark, are superb.

This is the Cam Fell Road; until recently an old milestone recorded the distance between Settle and Hawes from this spot, and coaches rattled this way until newer roads were built in the valley bottom at the beginning of the last century. It is also a Roman Road, one of Julius Agricola's campaigning roads between the forts at Bainbridge and Ribchester. The old road now carries part of the Dales Way on its 81 mile journey between Ilkley and Windermere.

Descend the track, easy, pleasant walking, superb views throughout, to Gearstone. Cross the footbridge across Gayle Beck – the infant River Ribble – and follow the track uphill to the main road. Although for years walkers have made their way back down Thorns Gill past Capnut Cave to the bridge, the status of this path on the Definitive Map has yet to be resolved. Walkers are therefore best following the main road past Gearstones, at least keeping to the grassy verges of the open common land, to avoid the ever present dangers and intrusion of fast moving traffic, and heading for Ribblehead station.

# Ingleborough

*This noble peak, one of the finest mountains in England, never disappoints, offering spectacular dramatic views at any season of the year. The ascent from Clapham, which includes Clapdale, Trow Gill and Gaping Gill, is rich in scenic and geological interest. Time required: 3½ hours.*

*Terrain: Stony paths and tracks, extremely steep in places.*

*Parking: Large car park by the National Park Centre in Clapham.*

*Public Transport: Leeds-Skipton-Lancaster railway to Clapham station (1¼ miles from village); Ribble 279/280/281 Skipton-Settle-Ingleton-Lancaster bus service direct to Clapham village.*

*Refreshment: New Inn pub and choice of cafes in Clapham.*

*Map: OS Outdoor Leisure Sheet 2 (Yorkshire Dales Western Area).*

CLAPHAM, that most delightful of Dales villages, has lost its roaring traffic on the A65, but has a good direct bus service from Ingleton and Skipton. It also boasts a railway station on the Leeds-Morecambe line, making it especially easy of access by fast train from West Yorkshire. The Information Centre by the car park has excellent displays of the area, the Reginald Farrer Trail leaflet, and helpful and informed staff. Cafes, pubs and a well supplied post office/shop cater for the needs of ramblers before and after a walk.

From Clapham village centre and car park cross the beck by the footbridge, make your way above the church to the top of the village (fine view of the waterfall), and bear left to the entrance of the Ingleborough Estate through the woodyard right. A small toll is payable for the entrance to the Estate grounds; this can be avoided by taking the bridleway around the back of the dale to Clapham Farm, but this has nothing of the charm and interest of the estate path, though woodlands and by the lake, which now forms part of the Reginald Farrer Trail – leaflet on sale at the Information Centre or Estate entrance.

The attractive woodlands, still containing a number of exotic species introduced by the great Clapham botanist and plant collector Reginald Farrer, surround the gorge of Clapdale, past an ornamental grotto, to the entrance of Ingleborough Cave, a deservedly popular and the oldest show-cave in the Dales. Regular guided tours leave the entrance at main holiday times and weekends in the summer months. Dry and well lit, it has a number of fantastic and quite beautiful formations which give insight into the incredibly rich and

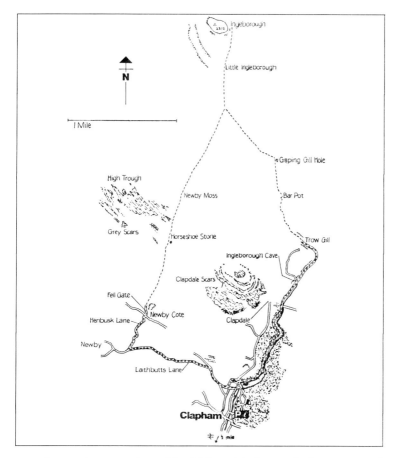

complex underground world which exists beneath the scars and crags of Craven.

Continue on the track to climb up Trow Gill, a steep, rocky and narrow dry valley, undoubtedly once an overflow channel for the streams that gouged out Ingleborough Cave. The limestone crags have a brooding, romantic appearance, a kind of Wolf's Glen, without wolves and marksmen, but no less atmospheric for that. Follow the path which continues from the summit, by the wall along a deeply eroded path, ignoring the first stile left but crossing the second. This leads to the edge of Bar Pot, a pothole of charm, before bearing across open pasture to Gaping Gill, and along the worn path to the fenced area of Gaping Gill Pot itself.

Despite its modest appearance, Gaping Gill is one of the wonders of Yorkshire, a vast internal chamber, with Fell Beck pouring down a vertical shaft 365 feet deep, into a space big enough to contain York Minster. Take great care around the slippery edge of the chasm; several people have slipped to certain death in recent years. On Bank Holidays it is often possible to be winched down the Gill by one of the local caving teams; the old adage is that they'll take you down for nowt, you only pay for the ride back!

Continue on the well defined track, boggy in places, towards the mountain peak, ascending steeply across the contours to the first "Summit" of Little Ingleborough, the gradient for the final craggy ascent through the gritstone outcrops and remains of a prehistoric wall to the summit plateau. In Iron Age and Romano-British times, Ingleborough mountain was a hillfort; after you visit the summit cairn and shelter, look for the clearly decipherable hut circles in the sandy peat. And the views, if you are fortunate to have a clear day, are glorious in every direction, as far as the Lancashire coast, the Lakeland peaks, the Bowland Fells and the sister peaks. Little wonder that until the end of the 18th century Ingleborough was considered the highest peak in Britain.

Unless you decide to go on to Ingleton or Chapel-le-Dale (see Walk 31), retrace your steps to Little Ingleborough summit. From here, keep directly ahead, almost due south-east along a faint path over the rough, open fell. As the gradient eases, look for the line of Grey Wife Sike and a series of potholes on Newby Moss, to the left of the limestone crags and pavement on High Trough and Grey Scars. A free-standing limestone boulder is marked on the map as Harryhorse Stone. The path is marked by shooting "hides". As the scatter of farm buildings at Newby Gate comes into view make directly for it, soon picking up deep sledge grooves around the intake walls down to the gate and enclosed way at Newby Cote.

The quickest way back to Clapham village is to go left along the quiet, high lane which offers attractive views across the Wenning Valley and Bowland. But slightly more interesting is to cross the lane and descend Henbusk Lane to Newby. As this lane swings sharp left into Newby village, with its charming village green, look for a green way which starts to the left of the unenclosed waste ground left, as a stream. Go over a low hurdle, into a delightful green way. This is Laithbutts Lane, the pre-turnpike highway between Newby and Clapham village. It is now somewhat wet underfoot after rain, with several small streams sharing the ancient way by the farm, Laithbutts. Pass the farmhouse and keep alongside the hedge to the right, to the gate. The way is now open across fields to another gate and pleasant enclosed way, meeting the lane just a few hundred metres west of Clapham village.

# Norber and Crummackdale

*This is a walk particularly rich in geological interest, including the famous Norber Erratics and spectacular limestone escarpments and pavements of Crummackdale. Time required: 4¹/₂ hours.*

*Terrain: Stony paths and moorland tracks, extremely steep in places.*

*Parking: Large car park by the National Park Centre in Clapham.*

*Public Transport: Leeds-Skipton-Lancaster railway to Clapham station (1¹/₄ miles from village); Ribble 279/280/281 Skipton-Settle-Ingleton-Lancaster bus service direct to Clapham village.*

*Refreshment: New Inn pub and choice of cafes in Clapham.*

*Map: OS Outdoor Leisure Sheet 2 (Yorkshire Dales Western Area).*

FROM the car park in Clapham, walk to the top of the village, continuing along the track to the right of the church. This is Thwaite Lane, soon swinging under two ornamental tunnels carrying the pre-turnpike road underneath and out of sight of the Ingleborough Hall Estate. The lane climbs steeply, past woodland and the junction with Long Lane, soon offering the familiar skyline of the Bowland Fells right. Follow the lane as it climbs over Thwaite Top, before descending towards Austwick. A ladder stile, left, leads to a grassy path towards the massive bulk of Robin Proctor's Scar ahead.

As you cross the pasture, note the strange, oval enclosure to your left – this is the site of Thwaite Tarn, an ancient glacial lake drained early last century. Take care to fork right before the scar, making for the wall-corner right and a ladder stile. You are now in a boulder-field – the dark, jagged boulders are the famous Norber Erratics, ancient Silurian rocks removed and carried by the Crummackdale glacier and deposited as the ice melted.

At the signpost, take the narrow way, left, through the limestone crags up to the plateau; a remarkable sight awaits you – scores of these great boulders, some perched precariously on a narrow pedestal of limestone as if only placed there yesterday and not by the last Ice Age. With their coverings of pale green lichens they look like fossilised creatures – northern iguanas petrified on this high plain.

Enjoying the fine views, return to the lower path, turning left towards Austwick and making for the ladder stile in the wall above Nappa Scar ahead. Cross, making for the gap above the scar, when above the springs, a great limestone crag, or what geologists describe as an uncomformity, overlies Ordovician slates with strange

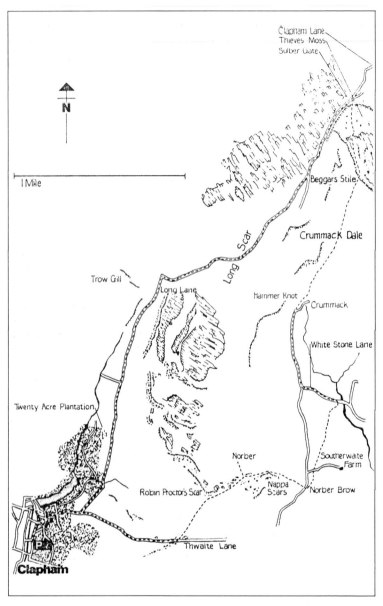

"conglomerate" rocks – a kind of geological concrete – wedged as the filling of the sandwich.

Continue along the top of the green ridge to the ladder stile to

Norber Brow. Cross the lane, over the next ladder stile, turning left over a wooden stile to the next ladder stile across a field. Cross the tarmac track to Southerwaite Farm, keeping straight ahead (ladder stile tip just visible on the horizon) up rough pasture, by a spring. Cross the stile, now descending across outcrops of slatey Silurian rock (more typical in the Lake District than the Dales) down to a stone step stile in the wall below left. Ahead a slab bridge and, in White Stone Lane, a delightful clapper bridge across the fast-moving Austwick Beck.

Follow this stony lane, left, to its junction with Crummack Lane. Ignore the ladder stile, right, but turn right along the lane up to Crummack Farm. Before this track swings right into Crummack Farm gate, keep ahead on a less distinct path outside the farm wall, through a gate, above the farm. Keep alongside the wall to a stile. Cross. The path now ascends the top of Crummackdale, above the surging torrent of Austwick Beck Head springs, by a green pasture.

You are now entering a spectacular area, limestone scars on all three sides, crag rising upon crag, Moughton Scar on the right, Long Scar left, and as you approach Beggar's Stile, bearing right off the Land Rover track to the ladder stile, ever more spectacular formations. Notice the remains of an ancient, obscure, supposedly Iron Age, but perhaps a Viking, "shiel" or sheepfold. Cross the stile, climbing up into a lunar landscape of white limestone pavement, the way threading between the formations. The massive shape of Ingleborough summit looms ahead. The path veers left, into a high, peat-covered corrie, Thieves Moss; this is a true mountain landscape, wild, bleak, on a heroic scale. At the left hand of the rim of the corrie is a narrow pedestrian gate – follow the stony path up to it.

Through this gate is a green track and another gate and stile; this is Sulber Gate (gate meaning road) which continues, across the Sulber Nick path between Horton and Ingleborough, to Selside. Cross the stile to enjoy splendid views across Sulber to Penyghent and Fountains Fell.

But to return to Clapham, go left along Sulber Gate, in a shallow valley by Long Scar. This pleasant green way soon forks – look for a small cairn. Your route swings right, green and pleasant – this is Clapham Lane – keep to the older more obvious way, avoiding Land Rover tracks off left. This path goes right, down into the top of Clapdale, to a gate and stile. You are now above the dark and brooding gorge at Trow Gill, and Ingleborough Cave at Beck Head and Clapdale Wood – all visible from this high level route.

Clapham Lane, now enclosed, becomes Long Lane – straight, pleasantly partially enclosed. The track dips across the line of the North Craven Fault by plantations before meeting Thwaite Lane. Right, downhill, through the tunnels and into Clapham village.

# Ingleton Glens and Kingsdale

*The finest waterfall walk in England, through Ingleton's romantic glens, can be continued through the wild landscape of Kingsdale. Time required: 2 or 4½ hours.*

*Terrain: Stony paths and tracks, extremely steep in places.*

*Parking: Large car park by the Community Centre in Ingleton.*

*Public Transport: Ribble 279/280/281 Lancaster-Ingleton-Settle-Skipton bus service to Ingleton.*

*Refreshment: Choice of pubs and cafes in Ingleton.*

*Map: OS Outdoor Leisure Sheet 2 (Yorkshire Dales Western Area).*

INGLETON, that attractive little Dales town under the magnificent outline of its famous mountain, and close to the spectacular waterfalls, is another excellent walking centre. It is well supplied with shops, cafes, pubs, and the Ingleton Community Centre has a small Information point. Pennine Motors and Ribble operate a regular bus service to Ingleton from Lancaster, Settle and Skipton, whilst motorists will find the village car parks well signed from the main A65.

Ingleton Glens form part of a private estate. The footpath through them is not a right of way, and a small charge is made for entry. The entrance to the Glens is at the bottom of the village, below the huge, disused railway viaduct that carried the former Ingleton-Tebay line. If coming by car, either park in the car park by the Community Centre at the top of the village, or take advantage of the all-in car park and entrance facility by the Black and White Cafe at the Glens entrance.

A walk through the waterfalls is easy to follow, but a word of warning. More lives have been lost here in recent years than anywhere in the Dales under or above ground; keep to the paths, which are perfectly safe, and take particular care to keep children under control. The gorges are steep and the current swift, and to fall in is to risk almost certain drowning.

Follow the riverside path through two small pedestrian gates, soon entering the deep limestone gorge of Swilla Glen, the River Twiss falling through a series of splendid torrents through delightful woodlands of yew, oak, hazel, pine and rowan. At Manor Footbridge, cross to the far side of the river, climbing up the gorge, past another gate, to Pecca Falls, where the river exposes ancient slates beneath the limestones – particularly noticeable are the pre-

104

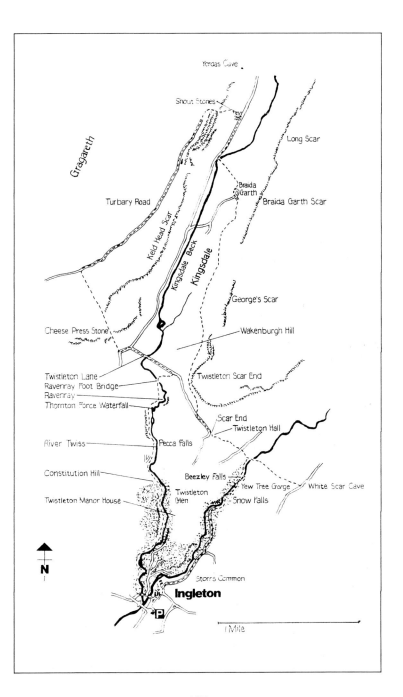

Yordas Cave

Shout Stones

Long Scar

Gragareth

Braida Garth

Braida Garth Scar

Turbary Road

Keld Head Scar

Kingsdale Beck

Kingsdale

George's Scar

Wakenburgh Hill

Cheese Press Stone

Twistleton Lane
Ravenray Foot Bridge
Ravenray
Thornton Force Waterfall

Twistleton Scar End

Scar End
Twistleton Hall

River Twiss

Pecca Falls

Constitution Hill

Beezley Falls

Yew Tree Gorge

White Scar Cave

Twistleton Manor House

Twistleton Glen

Snow Falls

N

Storrs Common

**Ingleton**

P

1 Mile

Cambrian Ingletonian Slates 100 metres below the falls, which are, in effect, a series of shallow potholes. Cross the Pecca Falls bridge, climbing into the open, swinging round towards Thornton Force, one of the most splendid picturesque waterfalls in England, 46 feet high over a limestone crag overlying ancient slates. With care you can scramble up to the falls, and behind the falls, to enjoy a shimmering curtain of water.

Continue above the falls to Ravenray footbridge to the pedestrian gate above. For those wishing to return directly to Ingleton, turn right along the green lane to Beezley's (4½ miles).

But for the full walk, to include Kingsdale, turn left down to the ford and footbridge across what is now Kingsdale Beck up to the lane. Turn left, but almost immediately, on the right, is a ladder stile. Cross this. The path, not clear on the ground, climbs at right angles to the wall, directly up, climbing steeply up, scrambling over clints – another ladder stile directly ahead marks the line of path up past the Cheese Press Stone, one of many huge scattered boulders. Cross, keeping straight ahead, but veering slightly right towards the wall right. Climb up, the gradient easing over rough pasture on to the wild plateau.

Soon a crossing track will come into view – bear right along it to a gate. This is the Turbary Road, an ancient road which, as its name implies, was used for collecting peat. It provides a fine, high level path above Kingsdale, along the shoulder of Gregareth. Follow the Turbary Road through gates, and gates and stiles. At the fifth gate, a walled enclosure contains Rowten Pot, a massive fissure in the mountainside, roaring with water. Continue to the next gate along, by the wall, leaving the track to bear right down across the next pasture across shallow scars to the gate below at Shout Stones on to the Kingsdale road; not a right of way but a well established permissive route.

Kingsdale, a wild lonely valley crossing the high pass between Whernside and Gregareth, has a strong Scottish Highlands flavour; remote, grand and bleakly lovely. The views of Whernside are superb. Turn right back along Kingsdale for 500 metres to where a stile gives access to the narrow footbridge across Kingsdale Beck. Cross the field ahead, climbing up to Braida Garth Farm, descending a hollow before the farm to the farm gate. Through here, crossing the main farm track, but turn left into an enclosure by the concrete and asbestos barn. A stile at the far side of this garth leads to a field path, through the gate ahead, then across a series of ladder stiles below Braida Garth Scar and Woods.

The path veers slightly – look for the ladder stiles, across a series of enclosures, below a lime kiln, above a wall, before swinging left up the edge of a shallow dry valley to Twistleton Scar End, at a small enclosure, before joining the green track of Kirky Gate descending from Whernside. Left here to Scar End Farm at Twistleton Hall. Keep ahead on the stile (signed Beezley Falls) with the farm buildings on the right across the fields to the road. Cross, down the track to Beezley Farm, and through the farmyard gate. (A path directly ahead crosses the river by the stepping stones and ascends the wallside to White Scar Show Caves, one of the largest and most interesting show caves in the North, and well worth a visit.) Otherwise the path from Beezley Farm descends left across the fields to the River Greta.

You now follow another splendid series of waterfalls and cataracts, past Beezley Falls, Yew Tree Gorge with its viewing bridge, down steps, crossing the footbridge above ancient slates in often dramatic juxtaposition, and verges rich in botanic interest, with orchids, violets, cowslips, herb robert. As you descend past the quarries, you see fine exposures of slates, with bands of quartz, remnants of limestone quarries and kilns – industrial scars slowly healing back into the landscape. A kissing gate leads to a stony track to the centre of Ingleton town.

# Ingleborough, Chapel-le-Dale and Twistleton Scars

*A popular ascent of Ingleborough from Ingleton town, which also offers a spectacular return walk past historic Chapel-le-Dale and over limestone pavement to Twistleton Scars. Time required: 4 or 6½ hours.*

*Terrain: Stony paths and moorland tracks, extremely steep in places.*

*Parking: Car park by the Community Centre in Ingleton.*

*Public Transport: Ribble 279/280/281 Lancaster-Ingleton-Settle-Skipton bus service to Ingleton; a convenient return can be made from Chapel-le-Dale by catching the train from Ribblehead station (1½ miles).*

*Refreshment: Choice of pubs and cafes in Ingleton; The Hill Inn at Chapel-le-Dale welcomes walkers.*

*Map: OS Outdoor Leisure Sheet 2 (Yorkshire Dales Western Area).*

FROM Ingleton town centre and car park make your way along the Hawes road, B6255, past the junction with the Old Road to Clapham to the edge of Storrs Common, before bearing right along the stony track across the common known as Fell Lane which soon goes through a gate to become an enclosed way climbing steeply between walls.

This is a popular, well-used path – look for a large rock embedded in the wall side about 300 metres along the enclosed way, which is known, for some reason lost in antiquity, as "Giant's Grave". Still climbing, the lane becomes an open track up past the picturesque Crina Bottom Farm, with fine views of the summit now ahead. You climb past Ranty Hole and Greenwood Pot, alongside the little valley of Hard Gill before the really severe, direct climb up peaty hillside and finally rough boulders, past high limestone scars, on to the craggy, steep face of the gritstone cap that forms the summit.

Views from the summit plateau are, in clear weather, magnificent. Give yourself time to explore the hut circles and remains of Iron Age defensive walls. Unless you plan to return directly to Ingleton, the route to Chapel-le-Dale is not that shown on all but the most recent OS maps which falls off the sheer cliff of the north face (The Arks), but bears at a more rational gradient off the north-west corner, Swine Tail, marked by a cairn.

Descend to a stile in the wall below, turning sharp left downhill,

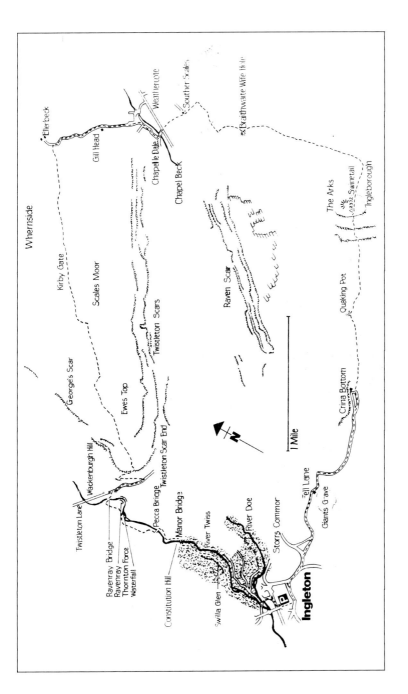

descending swiftly across the contours, over rough pasture, to a stile in the wall. Bend slightly right by Braithwaite Wife Hole and the line of path through a notch in the scar down to Souther Scales, bearing left at the farm through stiles to join the B6255 road at Chapel-le-Dale. Cross the road and follow the lane to Chapel-le-Dale. The church here, St. Leonards, originally 17th century, though rebuilt, is particularly lovely. The Lakeland poet, Robert Southey, wrote in 1847 that "A hermit who might wish his grave to be as quiet as his cell, could imagine no fitter resting place." Ironically in the 1870s, nearly 100 navvies, perishing from accidents, illness and disease in the building of Ribblehead viaduct and Blea Moor tunnel on the Settle-Carlisle line, were buried in an extended graveyard at Chapel-le-Dale. A marble plaque in the church commemorates the tragic deaths.

Follow the lane uphill past Hurtle Pot (visible from the lane). Wethercote Cave near here (no public access) was painted by Turner and formed the basis of one of the famous engravings for Whitaker's *Richmondshire*. Continue up the lane, past an unusual metal sculpture, and attractive woodland, up past Gill Head and towards Ellerbeck Farm. Before Ellerbeck bear left, uphill, along a track which swings across Blake Bank Moss. This is the ancient Kirby Gate, the old packhorseway between Ingleton and Kirby Stephen, following the high fell edge along the shoulder of Whernside.

The way climbs steadily, with open and dramatic views across Twistleton Dale and the limestone scars that skirt Ingleborough. You soon reach an area of extensive limestone paving. The way is now less obvious to follow, but gradually veers towards the fell wall, right, coming down from Whernside summit. As you approach Ewes Top the way becomes much more distinct, finally breaking through Twistleton Scar End in a deep and ancient limestone groove, with the woods and town of Ingleton below, and beyond the hills of Bowland. On a clear day the glint of the coast – Morecambe Bay – is visible from this point.

Follow the green path zig-zagging downhill to Twistleton Lane. Turn right in the lane, but through a well-used stile to the left go down to Ravenray Bridge and the famous and ever beautiful waterfall walk and past Thornton Force, Pecca Falls and Swilla Glen, back into Ingleton (see Walk 30). Do not forget to pay your admission toll at the entrance.

# THE NORTH'S LEADING PUBLISHER
# FOR MORE THAN 40 YEARS

Here is a selection of other books which may interest you:

COMPLETE DALES WALKER VOL I: NORTHERN DALES
(ISBN 1 85568 070 X)

DALES WAY
(ISBN 1 85568 072 6)

A WALK THROUGH THE YORKSHIRE DALES
(ISBN 1 85568 047 5)

YORKSHIRE DALES STONEWALLER
(ISBN 1 85568 049 1)

With over 150 books to choose from the Dalesman range
covers subjects as diverse as:

WALKING, WILDLIFE, HUMOUR, TOPOGRAPHY
ANTHOLOGIES, HOLIDAY GUIDES, GHOSTS and SPORT

For a catalogue of all the Dalesman titles send a SAE to:

DALESMAN PUBLISHING CO LTD
CLAPHAM, VIA LANCASTER, LA2 8EB